ORIGINS OF THE AMERICAN NAVY

Sea Power in the Colonies and the New Nation

Raymond G. O'Connor

UNIVERSITY
PRESS OF
AMERICA

Lanham • New York • London

Copyright © 1994 by

University Press of America®, Inc.

4720 Boston Way
Lanham, Maryland 20706

3 Henrietta Street
London WC2E 8LU England

Library of Congress Cataloging-in-Publication Data

O'Connor, Raymond Gish.
Origins of the American Navy : sea power in the colonies and the new
nation / Raymond G. O'Connor.
p.   cm.
Includes bibliographical references and index.
1. United States—History, Naval—To 1900.   2. United States.
Navy—History.   I. Title.
E182.026   1993   359'.00973—dc20   93–17839 CIP

ISBN 0–8191–9161–2 (cloth : alk. paper)

The paper used in this publication meets the minimum requirements of
American National Standard for Information Sciences—Permanence
of Paper for Printed Library Materials, ANSI Z39.48–1984.

To the Memory of Sally Sayles O'Connor
A Woman for all Seasons

Contents

Preface

This book is a study of the factors and circumstances that led to the establishment and development of an American Navy, and of the role of sea power in the winning of independence and the protection and promotion of the national interest during the early years of the Republic.

The emphasis throughout is on the making and execution of naval policy. This policy was formulated by the various administrations and Congresses in response to threats and dangers from abroad in an age of international anarchy. The nature and degree of response often was a matter of controversy among the branches of government, which reflected political, economic, sectional, and ideological differences. Presidential leadership was an essential factor in the creation of a navy, and John Adams, writing in his later years to his former adversary Thomas Jefferson, said that he "always believed the navy to be Jefferson's child." In fact, the navy was the child of many fathers, and it proved a dutiful offspring by upholding the sovereign rights of the fledgling nation.

Portions of this book have profited from readings by Professor John B. Hattendorf, Ernest J. King Professor of Maritime History at the Naval War College, Dr. William J. Morgan, retired Senior Historian in the Naval Historical Center, and Francis A. O'Connell.

Any errors of commission, omission, or interpretation are the responsibility of the author.

Raymond G. O'Connor

Chapter 1

The European and Colonial Experience

The men who created the American Navy were not operating in a vacuum or without benefit of maritime experience, direct or vicarious. The New World was discovered and colonies were established, developed, and maintained in the crucible of sea power. Appendages of the mother country, their umbilical cord was the highway of the seas nourished by the imperatives of the mercantilist system, with prosperity and actual survival depending on England. This reliance on sea borne commerce made them especially vulnerable to blockade or interdiction of trade. Each of the original thirteen colonies bordered on the sea and relied to a greater or lesser extent on its utilization for sustenance and livelihood. Militarily, the sea was both an asset and a liability—a protective moat against land invasion but a lifeline that could be severed or disrupted by a sufficiently powerful foe. Possessing some of the advantages and disadvantages of an insular nation, the colonies were hostages to the ships and seamen of the merchant marine and Royal Navy that roamed and protected the sea lanes in the Atlantic.

The founders of the American nation were products of this environment. They lived in an age of exploration, exploitation, settlement, and an imperial rivalry that had begun in the fifteenth century and reached its culmination in their lifetime. For three hundred years Europe had been seething with political, economic, cultural, religious, and technological changes, and the

1

events that accompanied these changes were a significant part of the heritage of the leaders of the American Revolution. Among these changes were: the consolidation of the nation-state with sufficient resources to support expensive ventures; the diversion of trade from the eastern Mediterranean to new routes that led to the riches of Asia; the Portuguese development of a seagoing vessel, the caravel; the introduction of navigational instruments such as the compass, the astrolabe and cross-staff, and accurate clocks to determine direction and position by celestial observation; improvements in map making as cartography became a respected profession; and the invention and use of movable type to permit the printing and wider distribution of knowledge about the world. The means to carry out ambitious enterprises abroad combined with the imperatives of wealth and power, propagation of the Faith, and the lack of unclaimed land in Europe to stimulate in the sixteenth and seventeenth centuries a race for routes and territory that rocked Europe to its foundations.[1]

The ocean, which had been an awesome and formidable barrier for thousands of years, became a thoroughfare that linked a luxury hungry Europe with the treasures of Asia and the Western Hemisphere. The Iberian nations established overseas empires as the rulers of Portugal cooperated with merchants to enhance trade, and Spain plundered the civilizations of Mexico and Peru. England, driven from the Continent by France and beset by civil turmoil, found stability under Henry VII and began to compete in the quest for markets and territory. The British Royal Navy, fostered by Henry VIII, truly came of age during the reign of Elizabeth I as the English sea hawks raided the Spanish treasure fleets, sought the Northwest passage to the Far East, staked out land for colonization, and climaxed its efforts by defeating the Spanish Armada in 1588. Without too much exaggeration, Sir Walter Raleigh could rightly claim that "he who rules the sea, rules the commerce of the world, and to him that rules the commerce of the world belongs the world itself."

The repulse of the Armada with its dramatic encounter of massive fleets caught the attention of every European nation and revealed a startling new dimension of sea power. The primary significance of the victory may have been, as one historian mentions, the demonstration that God was not necessarily on the side of the Catholics or of Spain. Nor did it end the contest between England and Spain, which continued for many decades. But militarily it revealed that faster and more maneuverable ships were effective in battle against the huge unwieldy galleons, and it proved the superiority of gunfire as a decisive weapon. Thus the way was opened to a shift from the earlier tactics of ramming and boarding followed by hand to hand combat to the tactics of ships in line of battle firing broadsides at the enemy. Many cannon were cast with the motto ULTIMA RATIO RE-GUM—the last argument of kings—as naval warfare was revolutionized.[2]

Yet the Elizabethans were not content to "kepe then the sea that is the wall of England," as *A Libel of English Policies* [c. 1436] put it. Visions of the New World promise stirred many Englishmen who viewed settlement in America as a solution to pressing ills that beset the homeland and as the most satisfactory method of participating in the race for empire. Richard Hakluyt, writing in 1584 in his *A Discourse Concerning Western Planting,* enumerated the advantages that would accrue to England by occupying this wilderness. Among them were spreading the Reformed Religion, replacing hazardous trading, reducing dependence on imports from other countries, providing employment, erecting bases to prosecute war with Spain, increasing Crown revenues and promoting the Navy, and finding the Northwest Passage to the Orient. As Samuel Eliot Morison wrote, "Here, one may say, are the blueprints for the British Empire in America from 1606 to 1776."[3]

England in its insularity may have had little choice in seeking greatness overseas. But the struggle with Spain that launched her on the road to empire was the product of a surge of energy that burst forth during the reign of the first Elizabeth to plant the seeds for a new nation in the Atlantic community and propel Britain to global leadership.[4]

The early English settlers in America became more aware of the crucial role of the sea in their lives than they had in their years of residence in England. Their dependence on the ocean was vividly revealed by the weeks spent on board frail sailing craft for the 3,000 mile journey, the ever present threat of enemy or pirate vessels, the establishment of settlements on or adjacent to the ocean, the importance of fishing for sustenance, and the vital factors of trade with and military protection from home. The adventurous or desperate souls who embarked on this enterprise maintained their ties with the mother country, and while few may have been seafarers at home many became so as they strove to master their new environment.

As the colonies spread along the coast they became more essential to the economic life of England, and the home government issued a series of regulations designed to promote self-sufficiency and maximum benefit for the nation. This mercantilist system was intended to create a balanced economy with the colonies providing goods, primarily raw materials, that could not be produced at home, while absorbing those finished items that England wished to export.[5] Of utmost importance were timber and naval stores used in the construction of ships. England had long been dependent on the Baltic countries as the major source for its ship building materials. Now the forests of North America offered relief from this dependence.

Significantly, the Navigation Acts, beginning in 1651, which imposed severe restrictions on trade, stipulated that colonial shipbuilders and owners should enjoy the same privileges as those in England. Thus encouraged, this industry developed rapidly in New England and produced vessels for colonial and mother country fishermen and merchants. In the construction of these ships the colonists established an initial component of sea power and provided the foundation for the American Navy since there was little difference in the design of merchant vessels and men of war. Both mounted cannon for encounters with pirates during peacetime and commerce raiding privateers or warships during war, and merchantmen served as combatants when so designated by the Crown.[6]

The English colonists had participated in all of these wars, and by charter they were held responsible for providing their own defenses against Indians or other enemies. Their militia had fought on land and in amphibious operations, notably in the capture of Louisburg in 1745, and their ships and crews had served as privateers or as part of the Royal Navy. While the colonies had no standing regular army or navy of their own, they were organized for mobilization and maintained a state of readiness to combat the natives or join their brethren in the European wars that radiated to holdings overseas.

The real or imagined wealth contributed by overseas possessions was almost an obsession with the courts of Europe, where it became an article of faith to believe that the destiny of nations would be determined by the nature and extent of colonial empires. The fulcrum of the balance of power, it was believed, rested in North America and the peripheral areas of the globe, with India looming as the great prize for the riches of Asia. Writing in 1758, Emerich de Vattel, the Swiss jurist, defined balance of power as "the arrangement of affairs so that no state shall be in a position to have absolute mastery and dominate over the others." While the word "absolute" may have been rejected by the statesmen of the time, they realized the degree to which a nation could dominate affairs. Increasingly they became convinced that international rivalry demanded a global approach with overseas appendages as the key to greatness if not mastery or domination.

The rise of England to a position of maritime preeminence was not the result of a conscious, deliberate, consistent long-range policy adopted by the government and pursued unremittingly over the centuries. Partly fortuitous, at times dictated by circumstances, the development of the Royal Navy was made possible by the presence of far-sighted statesmen in positions of authority at the right time. These statesmen prevailed in the dispute over whether England should adopt a "continental" or a "maritime" military strategy. Limited resources in men and materiel would not permit the luxury of both, and the colonists were first hand observers to and participants in the success of the choice that had been made.

England, as a result of its insular position, was compelled to become a seafaring nation. The concentration of its activities on the sea was manifest in government support of maritime and affiliated endeavors, which contributed to the welfare of the colonies and further revealed to the colonists the vital role played by sea power in their very existence. Yet the policy followed by Whitehall was not always calculated to inspire confidence among the settlers, who felt with some justification that they were being exploited by the home government with slight regard for their own concerns.[8]

The European contest for North America reached its climax in the Seven Years' War, 1756–1763, also known as the French and Indian War. This conflict attained global proportions, and it brought the colonists into the conflict more directly and to a greater extent than had been the case in previous European oriented struggles. The pursuit of their interests helped provoke the war and their enthusiasm for participation was comparably greater than heretofore. Moreover, the magnitude of the war placed strains on the mother country beyond its capacity and compelled it to draw more heavily on the colonies. The impressment of seamen that had provoked riots in Boston in 1747 met less resistance when the issue appeared less remote.

The Seven Years' War taxed Britain to its limits,[9] and all of her resources would have proved unavailing had it not been for the emergence of vigorous leadership and the implementation of an imaginative and revolutionary new military strategy. The war began badly for the English, with defeats on both land and sea, and displeasure brought a new leader to the helm of government, the elder William Pitt, Lord Chatham, the "Great Commoner." Thoroughly committed to the "maritime school," he supported his continental ally, King Frederick of Prussia, with funds, while employing his own forces in an "indirect" or "peripheral" strategy aimed at weakening the enemy at home and destroying his forces abroad. Calling on every segment of the Empire, Pitt marshalled his nation's efforts to strike at French trade routes, islands, bases, ports, and fleets.[10] Nor was this simply a strategy of attrition. Pitt concentrated the main British offensive in America to secure what he believed was the major objective of the war, namely, the North American colonies. The Caribbean and the Atlantic were the scene of amphibious or "conjunct" operations, commerce destruction and capture, and sea battles as England strove to sever France's lines of communication and maintain her own. By securing command of the sea and denying it to France, Britain was able to prevent the French forces from receiving logistic support while providing the troops and supplies necessary to sustain their armies and insure mobility of operations. Without this naval supremacy the outcome of the war undoubtedly would have been different. The lesson was not lost on the American colonists who perceived the alternative in vivid perspective.[11]

The Seven Years' War, in Francis Parkman's phrase, "made the Maritime and Colonial greatness of England." Further, it clearly established the Atlantic as the main artery of sea power. For centuries the maritime center of Europe had been the Mediterranean. But the opening of the New World presaged a shift, however gradual, to the west. The commercial value of the colonies had grown phenomenally to dwarf the trade with other areas, and the volume of shipping in the Atlantic had risen proportionately to become a major if not a determining factor in the prosperity of European nations. As the duc de Choiseul, appointed French Minister of Marine in 1761, wrote, "Upon the navy depend the colonies, upon the colonies commerce, upon commerce the capacity of a state to maintain numerous armies, to increase its population and to make possible the most glorious and most useful enterprises." Militarily, the Atlantic provided the logistic key to success in war by the interdiction of enemy commerce and supply. A new era had dawned.[12]

The growth of the colonial empires in the Western Hemisphere and the accelerating rate of trade not only enhanced the significance of sea power in commerce and war, but it imposed added strains on the rules governing the rights and duties of belligerent and neutral nations in regard to shipping during times of hostilities. The conflicts of the eighteenth century witnessed strenuous efforts to reach agreement on certain principles to be observed. At issue were: "(1) whether neutrals might enjoy a right to trade in innocent goods between port and port of an enemy power, including colonial ports, if the grant had not been made *bona fide* before the outbreak of the war; (2) the degree of protection to be enjoyed by neutral property and ships on the high seas; (3)

what constituted contraband; (4) what constituted legal block-ade."[13]

The major maritime powers, anxious to use their superior naval strength to greatest advantage against the enemy, had every reason to interfere with what the neutral nations consid-ered legitimate interests. Treaties designed to control belligerent activity on the high seas were often concluded between nations. But the interpretation or enforcement of the "law" regarding the rights of neutrals rested with the major naval powers, which usually took whatever action would contribute most to the weakening or destruction of the enemy. During the Seven Years' War dissatisfactions with the rules and practices relating to trade and blockade were exacerbated.[14] The British government for-bade trade with France, 1756–1761, and Spain, 1761–1763, in exploiting its maritime advantage. These regulations imposed hardships on the American colonies, which had enjoyed a lucra-tive trade with the Caribbean holdings of those nations. Many colonists felt that the home government was waging war against them rather than the proper enemy. Discrimination against colonial shipping continued until the onset of the American Revolution and contributed significantly to dissent.[15]

Interference with colonial shipping was only one legacy of the Seven Years' War that aggravated relations between the colonies and the mother country. The British government, heavily in debt, sought additional means to raise revenue by various forms of taxation and a vigorous attempt to enforce laws against smuggling, laws whose enforcement had been lax under a policy of "salutory," or "benign" neglect. Illegal trade, common even in time of war, had brought prosperity to the settlers. To have the Royal Navy interrupting this lucrative practice was degrading and financially detrimental to the colonies. Parliament seemed to feel that the colonies had not met their obligations in the recent conflict and was determined to exact penalties for alleged inadequate cooperation in furnishing troops, seamen, vessels, supplies, and a boycott of enemy commerce. The colonists resented what they considered an unfair attitude, for they be-lieved their contributions had been proportionate to their resources, consistent with their responsibilities, and much greater than in previous British wars.[16]

The accumulation of grievances that provoked revolt stemmed largely from a conflict that had freed thirteen colonies from a perennial French threat to their existence, and a disagreement over the sacrifices that had been made and should be made in order to provide security. The weakest links in the chain that bound the empire together had been exposed, and the elimination of a hostile neighbor gave the colonists a degree of security in defense that abetted their claims for a redress of wrongs.

NOTES

1. An admirable synthesis of scholarship is Samuel Eliot Morison, *The European Discovery of America: The Northern Voyages* (New York, 1971), although this writer disagrees with his statement that "in general, the navigational methods in effect around 1500 lasted, with many refinements but no essential changes, until 1920–30." 142. Actually, the problem of determining longitude was not solved until the middle of the eighteenth century with the development of an accurate clock, the chronometer. W. E. May and Leonard Holder, *A History of Marine Navigation* (New York, 1973), 157 ff. See also Morison's *The European Discovery of America: The Southern Voyages* (New York, 1974); John Horace Parry, *The Age of Reconnaissance, 1450–1650* (New York, 1963), and *The Spanish Seaborne Empire* (New York, 1966); Charles R. Boxer, *The Portuguese Seaborne Empire: 1415–1825* (New York, 1969), and *The Dutch Seaborne Empire* (New York, 1965); David Beers Quinn, *England and the Discovery of America, 1481–1620; From the Bristol Voyages of the Fifteenth Century to the Pilgrim Settlement at Plymouth: The Exploration, Exploitation, and Trial-and-Error Colonization of North America by the English* (New York, 1974); David B. Quinn and A. N. Ryan, *England's Sea Empire* (London & Boston, 1983); G. V. Scammell, *The World Encompassed: The First European Maritime Empires* (Berkeley, 1981). More specialized is Carlo M. Cipolla, *Guns, Sails, and Empires: Technological Innovation and the Early Phases of European Expansion, 1400–1700* (New York, 1966), where the author discusses new shipbuilding and ordnance techniques which, he contends, enabled Europeans to prevail over their non-western opponents.

2. Until the time of Henry VIII shipboard guns were light and were concentrated in the "castles" in the bow and stern. Henry wanted heavier guns mounted, and only the hull provided suitable platforms, so ports were cut in the sides to enable guns to be placed on the decks. Michael Lews, *The History of the British Navy* (Baltimore, 1957), 42–43. Sir John Hawkins "is,

perhaps, the first official exponent of the extreme doctrine of the use of purely naval action as the strategical policy of England, in opposition to the doctrine of the utilization of force on the Continent." Herbert Richmond, *The Navy as an Instrument of Policy, 1558–1727* (Cambridge, 1953), 30. Early English naval policy is well portrayed in G. J. Marcus, *A Naval History of England: The Formative Centuries* (Boston, 1961). Garrett Mattingly *The Armada* (Boston, 1959), is a classic in style and scholarship, and the ordnance of the opposing forces is analysed in Michael Lewis, *Armada Guns: A Comparative Study of English and Spanish Armaments* (London, 1961).

3. Morison, *The European Discovery of America: The Northern Voyages,* 560.

4. "English America was a land of many harbours, but its great rivers were navigable only to a line of falls and rapids a few score miles inland. These facts determined the shape of the settled territory that had come into existence by 1713." Ralph Davis, *The Rise of the Atlantic Economies* (Ithaca, N.Y., 1973), 264. This is an excellent survey of European and New World economic development from the sixteenth to the eighteenth centuries. For commercial rivalries between the colonial urban centers in the early eighteenth century, see Carl Bridenbaugh, *Cities in the Wilderness: The First Century of Urban Life in America, 1625–1742* (New York, 1938), 330–363. The discontents that motivated the early English immigrants are described in Carl Bridenbaugh, *Vexed and Troubled Englishmen, 1590–1642* (New York, 1968). Basically, they were seeking a higher standard of living and a more perfect society. The New World appeal to Englishmen is vividly portrayed in A. L. Rowse, *The Elizabethans and America* (New York, 1959).

5. Curtis P. Nettels, "British Mercantilism and the Economic Development of the Thirteen Colonies," *The Journal of Economic History,* XII (Spring 1952), 105–114.

6. The colonies provided wood for spars, oak for hulls and decks, pine for masts, and naval stores such as pitch, tar, rosin, and turpentine. The standard work is Robert G. Albion, *Forests and Sea Power: The Timber Problem of the Royal Navy, 1652–1862* (Cambridge, 1926); and recent studies include Arthur R. M. Lower, *Great Britain's Woodyard: British America and the Timber Trade, 1763–1867* (Montreal, 1973); and Charles F. Carroll, *The Timber Economy of Puritan New England* (Providence, RI, 1974). The Navigation Acts "were called upon to foster English shipping, to aid in training English-seamen, to develop English shipbuilding, and to preserve English trade." Lawrence A. Harper, *The English Navigation Laws: A Seventeenth-Century Experiment in Social Engineering* (New York, 1939), 377–378. For shipbuilding, naval stores, coastal and ocean trade in New England during the first half of the seventeenth century, see William B. Weeden, *Economic and Social History of New England, 1620–1789* (2 vols, reprint, New York, 1963), II, 573–594. One writer claims that "It is still a matter for debate whether the influence of sea power upon the growth of commerce has been greater than that of sea

commerce upon the development of navies." John U. Nef, *War and Human Progress: An Essay on the Rise of Industrial Civilization* (paperback ed., New York, 1968), 85–86.

7. "The most important complex of trade was that between Europe and the Americas." H. J. Habakkuk, "Population, Commerce and Economic Ideas," in A. Goodwin, ed., *The American and French Revolutions, 1763–93* (New Cambridge Modern History) (Cambridge, 1965), 33. See Max Savelle, "The American Balance of Power and European Diplomacy 1713–78," in Richard B. Morris, ed., *The Era of the American Revolution* (New York, 1939), 140–169. Savelle also pursues this theme in his *The Origins of American Diplomacy: The International History of Angloamerica, 1492–1763* (New York, 1967), 225 ff. A comprehensive treatment is Gerald S. Graham, *Empire of the North Atlantic: The Maritime Struggle for North America* (2nd ed., London, 1958).

8. "There was at that time [1740's] a great difference of opinion on the question as to whether we should direct our national strength towards colonial and maritime war or towards the maintenance of power in Europe." H. W. Richmond, *National Policy and Naval Strength and Other Essays* (London, 1928), 167. For a critical analysis of the vagaries of British naval policy, see Richmond, *Statesmen and Sea Power* (Oxford, 1946).

9. England became, officially, Great Britain in 1707 with the accession of Scotland.

10. The statesman "is that civil authority responsible for the maintenance of this [sea] power in peace and its effective use in war as a national weapon." *Ibid,* ix. The persistence of the Pitt approach in British strategic thinking was revealed in World War II when Winston Churchill repeatedly referred to its soundness in conversations with American military leaders, often to the annoyance of the latter.

11. The standard work is Julian S. Corbett, *England in the Seven Years' War: A Study in Combined Strategy* (2 vols, London, 1907). Also valuable is A. T. Mahan, *The Influence of Sea Power Upon History, 1660–1783* (Boston, 1890), 281–329. The English lost considerably more merchant shipping than did the French, but the latter were swept from the seas while English ship construction enabled trade to increase. Lawrence H. Gipson, *The Great War for the Empire: The Culmination, 1760–1763* (Caxton, ID, and New York, 1969), 71; E. H. Jenkins, *A History of the French Navy, From its Beginnings to the Present Day* (Annapolis, 1973), 140; Marcus, *A Naval History of England: The Formative Centuries,* 334. The latter claims that "In the final phase of the struggle Great Britain had no less than 8,000 merchantmen at sea and the supply of seamen appeared almost inexhaustable; the Navy alone employed 70,000 of them." *Ibid* 335. A comprehensive treatment is Richard Middleton, *The Bells of Victory: The Pitt-Newcastle Ministry and the Conduct of the Seven Years War, 1757–1762* (Cambridge, 1985).

12. Quoted in Gerald S. Graham, *The Politics of Naval Supremacy: Studies*

in British Maritime Ascendancy (Cambridge, 1965), 17. For the French perspective see James Pritchard, *Louis XV's Navy, 1748–1762: A Study of Organization and Administration* (Kingston, 1987). The economics of maritime supremacy are described in James F. Shepherd and Gary M. Walter, *Shipping, Maritime Trade, and the Economic Development of Colonial North America* (New York, 1972); and Judith Blow Williams, *British Commercial Policy and Trade Expansion, 1750–1850* (New York, 1972).

13. Samuel Flagg Bemis, *The Diplomacy of the American Revolution* (New York, 1935), 130.

14. For the Rule of 1756 by which England held that trade not open to nations in peace was not open in time of war, see R. Pares, *Colonial Blockade and Neutral Rights, 1739–1763* (Boston, 1938). A brief but authoritative survey may be found in A. Pearce Higgins, "The Growth of International Law, Maritime Rights and Colonial Titles, 1648–1763," in *The Cambridge History of the British Empire,* I, *The Old Empire: From the Beginnings to 1783* (New York, 1929), 538–560. A comprehensive treatment of the subject is P. C. Jessup and F. Deak, *Neutrality: Its History, Economics and Law,* I: *The Origins* (New York, 1935).

15. Oliver M. Dickerson, *The Navigation Acts and the American Revolution* (Philadelphia, 1951), 168–170.

16. "All told, Americans raised five times as many men as they had furnished in any other colonial war, to say nothing of 18,000 American seamen who swelled the Royal Navy." Don Higginbotham, *The War of American Independence: Military Attitudes, Policies and Practice, 1763–1789* (New York, 1971), 20. The contributions and colonists in the various wars are detailed in Douglas Edward Leach, *Arms for Empire: A Military History of the British Colonies in North America, 1607–1763* (New York, 1973).

Chapter 2

The First American Navy

The American Revolution must be viewed in the context of a series of armed conflicts. First as a civil war in which the colonists were seeking a redress of wrongs allegedly perpetrated by the King and Parliament; second, following the Declaration of Independence, as a war of national liberation; third, with France's entry, as the fifth in the Long series of Anglo-French wars; and fourth, after Spain and Holland became involved, as a global war in which Britain stood alone against a coalition of old and new enemies. Adding to Britain's distresses was the creation of the Armed Neutrality, whereby nonbelligerents joined to enforce their rights, as they saw them, to conduct "innocent" trade with all parties.

The mission of the Royal Navy following the Seven Years' War was to defend the Empire and enforce the laws, especially those regulating trade. Vessels were stationed off American ports to prevent the smuggling that had been practiced so assiduously by the colonists, who on occasion attacked the guarding patrols. Indignation appeared especially high in Rhode Island, whose inhabitants in 1764 fired upon a British schooner, in 1769 burned a sloop, and in 1772 destroyed another schooner. Although these actions could scarcely be termed the first engagements of the American Revolution, they reflected the intensity of feelings aroused by the stringent measures taken in the aftermath of the Seven Years' War. The protests and riots that occurred in opposition to impressment, the practice of forcing unwilling males to serve on board ship, revealed further discontent. Life at sea was at best unpleasant, and seamen often deserted. Replenishing the crew often involved coercive methods that violated what many believed to be the rights of Englishmen and inflamed the coals of revolt.[1]

The skirmishes at Lexington and Concord in April 1775 marked the beginning of the War of the Revolution, to be followed by the Battle of Bunker Hill, the investiture of Boston, and the creation of a Continental Army. The Massachusetts Third Provisional Congress initiated maritime operations on June 6, 1775 by appointing a committee that recommended the fitting out of six armed vessels to operate under the control of a Committee of Safety.[2] While this proposal was never implemented, the value of Massachusetts seaports and supplies was perceived by George Washington, who, although uncertain of his authority to do so, procured ships and manned them with soldiers from his army.[3] In supporting the siege of Boston these vessels disrupted the British supply lines, furnished the American forces with sorely needed provisions and munitions by capturing transports, and served as an important adjunct to the army until disbanded by order of the Continental Congress Marine Committee in 1777. When Washington moved to New York in the spring of 1776 he secured the assistance of the New York Committee of Safety in creating a smaller fleet for defending the water approaches. Although these ships were not employed in cooperation with the army, they did provide Washington with crucial supplies and proved to be an irritant to the British.[4]

Congress took its first formal action to wage naval warfare in a resolution of July 18, 1775 which exhorted "each colony, at their own expense" to "make such provisions by armed vessels" to protect themselves "against all unlawful invasions, attacks, and depredations from cutters and ships of war." Eventually local or state navies were established by all but two of the thirteen colonies (New Jersey and Delaware excepted) and usually consisted of smaller vessels for port, coastal and trade defense, or for commerce raiding. Designed primarily for inshore, harbor, and river operations, the state navies were ordinarily controlled by a committee of the legislative body.[5]

Washington's navy was established under his loose interpretation of his Congressional commission as commander "of all the continental forces." It was financed and controlled under this authority, and his first vessel sailed on September 5, 1775.[6] But a navy was not specifically authorized by Congress until later in the fall of 1775. The initiative came from the Rhode Island Assembly which, by resolution on August 26, 1775, instructed its delegates to the Continental Congress to urge that body to construct "a fleet of sufficient force for the protection of these colonies." Before this suggestion could be considered, and prompted by news that two military supply ships had sailed from England for Canada, the Congress, after vigorous debate, referred the question to a committee of three. Opposition to the establishment of a Continental Navy came largely from southern and middle state delegates, who contended that it was expensive and foolhardy to contest Britain's overwhelming maritime superiority. Nonetheless, Congress approved a committee recommendation and authorized Washington to secure two armed vessels from Massachusetts; on October 13 approved fitting out two warships; and on October 30 provided for two additional vessels.[7]

The same day the Congress added four members to the original committee of three, which became known as the "Naval Committee." Each represented a different colony in an effort, no doubt, to provide geographical distribution and avoid a charge of localism. Yet New Englanders predominated, with John Adams representing Massachusetts, Stephen Hopkins Rhode Island, Silas Deane Connecticut, and John Langdon New Hampshire. The other members were Christopher Gadsden of South Carolina, Richard Henry Lee of Virginia, and Joseph Hewes of North Carolina.[8]

The Naval Committee, initially enjoined only to investigate the cost of, report on, and supervise the fitting out of armed vessels, soon expanded its duties to assume responsibility for recommending legislation pertaining to all naval matters. Increasingly the Congress delegated authority to the Committee to issue appointments and sailing orders. The "Rules for the Regulation of the Navy of the United Colonies," was prepared mainly by John Adams using the British example. Approved by the Congress on November 28, 1775, it prescribed the behavior, treatment, and punishment that should prevail on board ship, and specified daily rations of food and rum.[9] Prompted by repeated appeals from Washington to clarify his jurisdiction in maritime affairs, the Committee submitted reports that were immediately adopted by the Congress approving Washington's naval actions, prescribing the allocation of prize money, and recommending that colonies establish admiralty courts to adjudicate cases on captured vessels and cargo.[10] On January 5, 1776, the Committee ordered its embryonic fleet, with Esek Hopkins as commander in chief, to proceed against British forces in Chesapeake Bay, off the Carolina coast, and off Rhode Island. Encountering obstacles, Hopkins sailed to the Bahamas to capture Nassau and then to Long Island Sound, where his units had an inconclusive engagement with a British ship that managed to escape.

In less than three months the Naval Committee had established, purchased, outfitted, and manned the first Continental Navy while promulgating the necessary directives, rules, regulations, and legislation for the prosecution of naval warfare. Its accomplishments would be considered remarkable under any circumstances. But the chaotic situation that prevailed in the colonies from a military, political, economic, and administrative point of view makes its achievements almost unique in the annals of bureaucratic efficiency.[11]

The apparent reluctance of the Congress to grapple with the problem of a Continental Navy can easily be understood, if not condoned, by considering the position in which this body found itself. First convened on September 4, 1774, and representing every colony except Georgia, it produced a Declaration of Rights and Grievances protesting British actions and legislated a boycott against the importation of British goods while still pledging allegiance to the King. The second Congress convened on May 10, 1775 after the clashes at Lexington and Concord, again with the purpose of seeking relief from the alleged oppressions of the British government. As military activity intensified, London rejected colonial appeals and the King declared the

colonies in rebellion. The Continental Congress, literally overcome by events, found itself functioning as a governing body
engaged in a civil war with the most powerful nation on earth.
Lacking constitutional legitimacy, and representing thirteen colonies each of whom was jealous of its prerogatives and distrust-
ful of any outside authority, the Congress was compelled to
evolve its own methods and procedures under the most adverse
circumstances.

In its first session, which lasted from May 10 to August 2,
1775, the second Congress concentrated on military affairs and
appointed a number of temporary committees to investigate and
recommend steps for the prosecution of the war on land. Resolutions exhorted the colonies to military and naval effort, created an army, authorized the issuance of paper money to finance
the struggle, and provided for limited trade.[12] Yet there was a
reluctance to take action that would provoke sterner measures
to suppress the rebellion and evoke a less compromising attitude
in London. When Congress reconvened in September 1775 the
delegates were informed that Washington had acquired some
vessels, were presented with the Rhode Island resolution, and
were advised of the departure of the British military supply
ships. Essentially, necessity forced the creation of a Continental
Navy. Without it the colonies could not protect ports or commerce, disrupt British communications, support the army, secure supplies by capture, or carry the war to the enemy. Still, it
is difficult to exaggerate the differences of opinion that prevailed
in Congress over the desirability or propriety of many of the
steps urged by the radical delegates, the delicate situation of
each state's autonomy, and the need for unanimity to secure
approval of resolutions. Debate was often long and bitter, involving local interests, expense, strategy, personalities, and
means as well as ends. Not only what should be done was often
at issue, but how it should be done, and experiments with
administrative organization often proved costly.

Although the Congress had purchased, outfitted, and manned
vessels, it was not until December 9, 1775 that this body considered the Rhode Island resolution. At this time a committee was
appointed "to devise ways and means for furnishing these colo-

nies with a naval armament, and report with all convenient speed." The Committee consisted of one member from each colony. An ad hoc committee submitted a report on December 13 urging the construction of thirteen frigates. Approving this recommendation on the same day, the Congress on December 14 appointed a permanent committee of thirteen members, one from each colony, to supervise construction and outfitting.[13] The Marine Committee, as this body came to be known, continued in existence until October 28, 1779, when it was succeeded by the Board of Admiralty. The original Naval Committee was permitted to function in connection with the fleet it had formed as an expedient measure, that is, the naval force under Hopkins. Then, on August 5, 1776, Congress resolved "that the Marine Committee be directed to order the ships and armed vessels belonging to the Continent, out on such cruizes [sic] as they shall think proper." Irregular attendance at meetings induced Congress to authorize, on June 6, 1776, a "board" of five members to constitute a quorum and conduct the Committee's business.[14]

The gradual if not leisurely approach Congress took in creating a Navy, in contrast to the urgency demonstrated in establishing a Continental Army, reflects the nature of the conflict as conceived by the delegates at different stages in the Revolution. More desperate measures were invoked as the King revealed his determination to crush the rebellion, and the colonists retaliated by escalating their military efforts.

A further decentralization of authority designed to relieve the Marine Committee of details, promote efficiency, and expedite activities, was provided by the establishment of two boards, one at Philadelphia and one at Boston. The former, the Navy Board of the Middle Department, was established by Congress on November 6, 1776 to control affairs in the middle states. To administer affairs in New England, the Navy Board of the Eastern Department was established on April 19, 1777. The duties of these boards were comprehensive. While functioning under the direction of and reporting to the Marine Committee and its successors, they came to exercise a great deal of autonomy in supervising the naval affairs of their districts. These duties included the acquisition, fitting out, and manning of vessels, and the convening of courts of inquiry and courts martial.[15] Only the board at Boston, however, was allowed to issue sailing orders, and this authority was given reluctantly because of the difficulty in communications with the Marine Committee. These boards performed valuable services during the period of growth and operation of the Continental Navy. But as the Navy deterioriated in 1780 and 1781 due to inefficiency, financial distress, and losses at sea, the boards were gradually dissolved.

Meanwhile, the Congress, reflecting a general dissatisfaction with the state of the Navy and continuing to experiment with administrative organization, replaced the Marine Committee on October 29, 1779 with a Board of Admiralty, with duties essentially the same as those of its predecessor.[16] Composed of three commissioners and two members of Congress, the Board of Admiralty proved inefficient and unwieldy and contributed to a growing controversy in Congress between two factions, those who advocated a delegation and concentration of power and those who believed in its continued dispersal in committees. Eventually the "concentrative" group prevailed, and on February 7, 1781 Congress established several offices including a Superintendent of Finance, a Secretary of War, and a Secretary of Marine. The latter was assigned most of the responsibilities held by the Board of Admiralty except for the movements of warships. When Congress failed to fill this post, the administration of naval affairs was gradually assumed by the Superintendent of Finance, Robert Morris. As temporary expedients Congress authorized the appointment of an Agent of Marine on August 29, 1781, and on September 7, 1781 placed this office under the Superintendent of Finance.

Morris was well qualified for the post because of his shipping interests, previous association with affairs of the Continental Navy, and ownership of privateers whose depredations during the Revolution had brought him substantial financial returns. He continued in this position until 1784 and proved to be a vigorous and conscientious administrator, while urging unsuccessfully that Congress provide for a larger Navy during the war and for the subsequent peace. In effect, however, he presided over the liquidation of the Navy as Congress directed the phasing out of the naval establishment and a settlement of accounts, both being effected by the Board of Treasury.[17]

Thus during the eight year struggle, the Congress created four agencies to cope with the complexities of maritime warfare. First, the Naval Committee, officially in existence from October 5, 1775 to December 14, 1775, but continued until January 1776 to complete its work; second, the Marine Committee, from December 14, 1776 to October 28, 1779; third, the Board of Admiralty from October 28, 1779 to July 1781; and fourth, the Agent of Marine in lieu of the intended Secretary of Marine from August 1781 until the final termination of naval obligations. This last office was never officially discontinued by Congress but it ceased to exist as all its functions were ended. The committee system of administration was consistent with the absence of an executive and the reluctance of Congress to delegate authority. It was, perhaps, even desirable in the early stages of the Continental Navy when experience and expertise were lacking and affairs were not so multifarious. As details increased, new problems emerged and membership changed, the complex decision making process revealed the shortcomings of the committee system.

Efforts to profit by the centralized British organization failed, as did the abortive attempt to set up a Secretary of Marine comparable to the British First Lord of the Admiralty, a civilian. No professional office was ever established equivalent to the British First Sea Lord or even to that of George Washington in the Army. Under the circumstances bureaucratic inefficiency was understandable, and it was compounded by the presence of novices and the uncertainties of communications by land and sea. Nonetheless, naval affairs would have been conducted more effectively and expeditiously if executive authority had been delegated to the most qualified individuals who would be held responsible and would report to the Congress or a committee. This was the case with the Board at Boston and, to a lesser degree, the Middle Board at Philadelphia. Efficiency in administration did increase, as noted, when Robert Morris as Agent of

Marine made decisions without having to convene a committee or worry about a quorum, each of whose members would have equal voice in determining any course of action.

The exact date on which the American Navy was "founded" is difficult to establish. Washington was the first to employ armed vessels against Britain, but without formal authorization. Congress never censured him and retroactively approved his actions. But the Congressional resolution of October 5, 1775, which first authorized the utilization of armed vessels "to be on the continental risque and pay," was the effective beginning of the Navy. The legislation of October 13, 1776, considered the "official" founding of the Navy, envisioned a "fleet" and was followed by resolutions providing for the commissioning of officers and the codification of rules governing naval activity. The appointment of the committee of seven and the authorization to purchase and outfit additional vessels on October 30, 1775 marked another significant development in the evolution of the Navy, and Morison considers that this date "is regarded as the birthday of the Continental and United States Navies." Not until December 13, 1775, however, did the Congress move to build a navy, and the following day to establish a permanent committee that eventually was delegated authority to supervise and direct naval affairs.[18]

A major obstacle in the attempt to create a navy was the dispute over how it should be employed. Washington, besieging British force in Boston on three sides by land, readily perceived the need to close the sea opening and acted accordingly. The Continental naval strategy evolved slowly and kept pace with the interest of Congress in maritime activities. Initially, the Navy was intended to aid the military effort on land by denying logistic support to the enemy, capturing badly needed supplies of weapons and powder, and preventing seaborne attacks. Defensive in nature, this policy left the initiative to the enemy, did not fully exploit the native seafaring abilities of the colonists, and avoided hurting Britain where she was most vulnerable, namely, her maritime jugular vein.

Again, events were to precipitate a change. The first action of an offensive nature was directed by the Naval Committee on

January 5, 1776. Esek Hopkins, now commanding a fleet of seven vessels, was ordered to sail for Chesapeake Bay. If investigation revealed that British strength was not "greatly superior" to his own, he was "immediately to Enter the said bay, search out and attack, take or destroy all the Naval Force of our Enemies that you may find there." If successful he was to proceed to North and South Carolina, eliminate British forces in that area, then sail to Rhode Island and "attack, take and destroy all the Enemies Naval force that you may find there." The Committee further authorized Hopkins to conduct other operations at his discretion "to distress the enemy" and to call on the colonies for aid.

Hampered by bad weather, Hopkins sailed to the Bahamas, where a landing force of marines and sailors captured New Providence Island with its principal town Nassau, which was defended by two forts. After loading his ships with munitions, Hopkins set course for Rhode Island. En route two British warships and two merchant vessels were captured, and a sharp engagement occurred with the *Glasgow*, a 20 gun frigate. Both sides suffered damage, including casualties, and Hopkins broke off the engagement in anticipation of his foe receiving assistance. Subsequently, Hopkins was dismissed from the service for disobedience of orders in not attacking the enemy in the Chesapeake, despite the latitude given by his instructions. The inability of his superior fleet to subdue the *Glasgow* probably was held against him.[19]

As hostilities intensified and the Crown seemed more determined to stamp out the rebellion without concessions and by invoking more extreme measures, the Congress decreed the waging of total war on the sea. A series of resolutions passed on March 23, 1776, justified on the grounds that Britain was waging war in a "lawless manner," provided that all British vessels and their contents, including cargo, were subject to capture by Continental warships, colonial armed vessels, and privately owned duly commissioned armed ships or privateers.[20] These seaborne predators pursued an aggressive strategy that jeopardized the enemy's oceanic and coastal trade routes, assaulted towns, disrupted logistical support for the British armies in

America, forced insurance rates and prices on imported items to rise drastically, and led to a further dispersion of the Royal Navy as warships were assigned to escort convoys and patrol the sea lanes. Cruising in the waters around England and even into the Channel itself, American armed vessels alarmed the populace, which clamored for more protection. Increasingly, British citizens supported an end to the war that had been denounced at home by a vocal minority since its inception, and that became less popular as it dragged on, expanded its dimensions, and became financially burdensome.

As a result of final Congressional commitment to virtual unrestricted preying on British commerce, many Americans became enthusiastic exponents of maritime warfare. In previous wars colonial privateers had served the British cause with good effect, bringing remarkable profits to ship owners and crews. The practice had reached its zenith during the Seven Years' War, so a large segment of the population of the seaport towns was prepared and eager to pursue this lucrative business of commerce raiding.[21] Congress, unwilling in the early stages of the war to extend this practice beyond the interdiction of military support, and aware that it was being conducted with either state or no authorization, had considered a resolution on November 25, 1775, that provided "no master or Commander of any vessel shall be entitled to cruize [sic] for or make prize of any vessel or cargo before he shall have obtained a commission from the Congress or from such person or persons as shall be for that purpose appointed in some one of the United Colonies."[22] At issue were two questions: first, to what extent should the colonies prosecute hostilities against the mother country when the objective was a redress of wrongs that some thought would best be secured by not pushing the Crown and Parliament too far; and second, the legality of commissioning privateers by a government that did not claim sovereignty.[23]

The commission consisted of a document which required the posting of a bond to insure against violations of instructions issued by the government regarding the conduct of privateers in the capture and disposal of "lawful" prizes. These instructions were based on the customs and practices, and occasionally a treaty, that prevailed in the eighteenth century among the European nations during time of war. Congress on November 25, 1775 considered regulations for the disposition of prizes confined to ships and cargo supporting the British armed forces. The resolution stipulated that the colonies should establish courts of admiralty, that commissions must be issued by the Congress or by a colony, and that privateers were entitled to all of the prize money while Continental or state vessels should share their gains with the respective governments.[24] When Congress took the ultimate step, on March 23, 1776, of authorizing the capture of all British ships and cargo, it followed with detailed "Instructions to Privateers" on April 3, 1776, to be supplemented by additional articles on April 7, 1781, with admonitions on the rights of neutrals and a more careful definition of contraband.[25]

There is some dispute over the commissioning, terminology, number, and effectiveness of these privately owned armed commerce raiders. Congress adopted a commission form to be completed and issued by the states, the commissioners in France, and designated agents in New Orleans and Martinique.[26] At times, the states accepted Congressional jurisdiction in the commissioning of these vessels. This was consistent with the international practice, which made privateering legitimate if it represented and was regulated by a sovereign government engaged in war. Otherwise capturing vessels treated the crews as pirates, as the British government initially was inclined to do. The term "privateer" applied to privately owned armed vessels devoted exclusively to raiding, whereas vessels carrying cargo, but also involved in the capture of prizes, were called "letters of marque" after the authorizations they received. Such a distinction was often blurred. The wording of the commission was virtually identical and the two categories were not separated in regard to legality, behavior, or record keeping.[27] The total number of these vessels commissioned during the Revolution is in some dispute, with one authority estimating 1,151 and another approximately 2,000.[28] No accurate total can be ascertained because of incomplete data, duplications, and the occasional switch of vessels and crews from one category to another—i.e., Continental, state, privateer. As Allen puts it, "there was to some extent a sort of blending of three classes of sea service, both as regards ships and personnel."[29] The informalities of American maritime warfare were indicative of the chaotic governmental structure that prevailed in the colonies and the disparate motives of the participants as idealism and long range objectives clashed with personal ambition amidst the vagaries of vacillating military fortune.

The contributions of the privateers to the outcome of the war are even more controversial. Recruiting for the Continental Navy was hindered by the promise of greater financial rewards in privateering, where all of the prize money went to the owner and crew. Furthermore, the privateers, operating with little direction, control, or coordination of movements, did not always observe the rights of neutrals or the regulations issued by Congress. Yet these privately owned, armed, and operated vessels inflicted incalculable damage on the enemy, capturing or destroying more than 2,000 British ships with their valuable cargoes. One may not agree that "it was this attack on England's commerce that struck the mortal blows to British supremacy in America—not Saratoga or Yorktown."[30] Nor with the other extreme that "The militia of the sea was as futile as the militia of the land. Both undermined the spirit of the Service and made difficult any thoroughgoing organization and discipline."[31]

While the privateers had a detrimental effect on the Continental Navy, especially in regard to recruiting, the Congress, primarily for financial reasons, was unable to establish and maintain a significant naval force. During the final years of the war the Continental Navy virtually ceased to exist, while privateering increased and ravaged British commerce with significant benefit to the colonies. The contribution of these quasi-official warships to the revolutionary cause was considerable if unmeasurable, both materially and psychologically, and they constituted by far the most substantive American maritime contribution to victory.[32]

The hostility of France and Spain toward Great Britain was demonstrated by their attitude toward American privateers. Both allowed the privateers to outfit and dispose of prizes in their ports in violation of the Treaty of Utrecht of 1713 and the

Treaty of Paris in 1763. Spain extended the hospitality to her colonial ports, while denying regular commercial privileges to the colonists. Efforts to secure the same concessions from Holland and Prussia were unsuccessful because these nations were less inclined to incur the wrath of England.[33] Operating from European ports, the American privateers ranged the sea lanes around the British Isles, in the North Sea and the Bay of Biscay, while New Englanders haunted the fruitful waters of Nova Scotia and Newfoundland. Other American predators cruised the balmy seas of the West Indies where much of Britain's trade was centered. Thus the enemy was attacked where it was most vulnerable.

Oddly enough, Alfred Thayer Mahan virtually ignores the activities of these maurauders in his writings on the maritime activities of the American Revolution.[34] No doubt his aversion to the *guerre de course* or commerce raiding method of employing naval power, stemmed from his espousal of a strategy that emphasized control of the sea. Victory in war, Mahan argued, could be achieved only by fleet action and the destruction of the enemy forces. Writing at a time when warships were undergoing drastic technological change and the United States was entering a new stage in world relationships, Mahan sought to apply his concept of the lessons of the past to what he conceived of as the needs of an America that, as he put it, was looking outward. In the context of his time and his perception of naval developments, with no awareness of the potentialities of submarine warfare, his thesis and outlook are understandable. Even the most visionary of Revolutionary leaders did not contemplate the destruction of the Royal Navy. The best that could be hoped for was coastal defense, primarily by the state and Continental navies, the interdiction of military supplies, and the disruption of trade by every variety of armed vessel that could be utilized.

The military strategy of the war evolved, or one might say grew, inadvertently. During the early stage of the war, the colonists became more determined to gain the concessions they sought and continued to place more power in the hands of Congress to coordinate and control military affairs. In the summer of 1775 the main effort was concentrated on the British army in Boston with Washington in command of the American forces. That same year two expeditions were launched against Canada to procure military supplies and gain support from the French populace. When the invasion was repulsed the American military strategy became one of attrition or, as one writer puts it, of erosion, namely, to continue fighting until the British government became sufficiently weary of the entire affair to concede the American demands.[35] Meanwhile, the colonies sought outside aid primarily from France, which furnished supplies clandestinely in an effort to weaken its perennial enemy.

The British government, failing to perceive the serious dimensions of the rebellion and reluctant to make a massive military commitment, concentrated on the Continental armies and employed its maritime strength to support the troops. As the conflict extended into 1776 debate ensued over the best method of subduing the colonists, with some urging a stringent blockade of colonial ports to stifle commerce and compel submission.[36] The Royal Navy had experienced a period of decline following the Seven Years' War, as could be expected in the euphoria of victory and the urge to reduce expenditures. The normal peacetime reduction in ships and personnel had been accompanied by a deterioration in the seaworthiness of vessels as hulls decayed and economy prevented proper upkeep and replacement. As the Revolution continued the Royal Navy and the British merchant marine suffered from being deprived of American naval stores, timbers, and masts, as well as the shipbuilding facilities that had produced nearly one third of the vessels registered in Britain in 1776.[37]

The problem of securing and maintaining crews continued to plague the British Navy. Some officers refused to serve, either out of sympathy to the American cause or owing to an unwillingness to fight against their fellow countrymen.[38] Recruiting seamen always had been difficult because of the hard life, the rigorous discipline, the low pay, and the hazards of battle. Bounties and the prospect of sharing prizes were inadequate compensations. Consequently, impressment became the most effective method of recruitment, although it depleted the merchant service of trained personnel and gathered a number of

misfits and incompetents from the dregs of British society. The
colonial sailors who had served in previous wars were now
denied to the British Navy by the rebellion, and the high inci-
dence of sickness that prevailed on ships remaining at sea for
any length of time further hampered the fleet's readiness for
war.[39]

By spring of 1776 indecision as to courses of action began to
give way to decisive steps by the British government and the
Continental Congress. A massive expeditionary force was
readied in England to crush the rebellion, but it was accompanied by peace commissioners who were empowered to negotiate
a settlement of the political and economic sources of discontent.
Delays in outfitting and transport prevented this expedition from
departing until June 1776, but by July Congress had voted for
independence. Although the dual offensive may have been a
mistake,[40] other factors also frustrated this maximum British
commitment to subdue the colonies.[41]

Delegates to the Congress carefully considered the implications of a vote for independence. This drastic escalation of aims
from the original petition for a redress of wrongs emerged
gradually as the Congress changed from an advisory to a governing body. Attitudes hardened toward Britain as the colonists
experienced the horrors and hardships of war, and moderate
delegates were replaced by extremists. Motives for independence varied among the delegates. But a factor in the minds of
some, at least, was the urgent need to secure support from other
nations. So long as the conflict remained a domestic squabble,
other governments had little incentive to adopt policies or practices that would provoke Britain to war.

Congress moved gradually toward an extreme position. As the
fighting resumed early in 1776, Congress refused to violate
British law by opening American ports to foreign trade and
foreign ships. Doing so would have been tantamount to a declaration of independence and the delegates were still committed
to the objective of securing a redress of wrongs. But on August
22, 1775 Parliament formally cut off all trade with the colonies.
Thus the need to reopen foreign trade furnished a strong impetus

for independence, since without commerce the colonies could not wage war or even survive.

The first affirmative step toward independence was the Congressional resolution of April 6, 1776 which opened trade with all the world except Great Britain. Two weeks later Congress authorized the capture of British shipping. Responding to rising sentiment and desperate for increased aid from France and other nations hostile to Britain, Congress on June 7, 1776 began to consider a resolution for independence that included a plan of confederation providing for "the most effectual measures for forming foreign Alliances."[42] A redrafted resolution was approved on July 2, 1776. The final Declaration of July 4 included the assertion that "as Free and Independent States" the United Colonies "have full power to levy War, conclude peace, contract Alliances, establish Commerce, and to do all other Acts and Things which Independent States may of right do." The Declaration was a plea for assistance in a struggle against tyranny, an appeal that may not have been attractive to the monarchs of Europe. Paramount was the prospect of depriving Britain of America, its most valuable colonial asset, what Chatham in November 1777 called "the fountain of our wealth, the nerve of our strength, the nursery and basis of our naval power." France and Spain supported the colonies in spite of the implications of successful colonial revolt for their own empires because they welcomed the opportunity to restore some of the power, prestige and wealth that they had lost in the previous decade.

As Congress labored to provide the sinews of war, hostilities continued with three major British offensives in 1776: (1) from Canada via Lake Champlain to follow up the repulse of the American invasion and squeeze Washington's army, which was to be driven north from New York by (2) the main British force; and (3) the capture of Charleston, South Carolina. The latter was frustrated by the determined resistance of the harbor forts, and the New York campaign began badly for the Americans because of the British troop strength and control of the water approaches.

Washington's education on the importance of sea communications, begun at Boston, continued as he retreated into New

Jersey and Pennsylvania. Washington's "naval genius" developed from his long experience of being thwarted by the mobility and flexibility enjoyed by the British forces. He never pretended to understand naval tactics or the fundamentals of seamanship. But he came to perceive the strategic role of sea power in land operations on or near the coast before many of his contemporaries. Washington's exasperation over British superiority at sea was revealed in a letter of July 25, 1777, when he complained that "The amazing advantage the Enemy derive from their Ships and the Command of the Water, keeps us in a State of constant perplexity and the most anxious conjecture."[43] Until France entered the war he could only fulminate against the advantages that Britain enjoyed from its domination of the sea. But the prospect of the French fleet joining in combined operations brought forth his most cogent thoughts on the matter.

Returning to the British thrust from Canada, the immediate objective was Lake Champlain. The terrain was virtually impassable and water transport was the only practicable means of conveying the army to its projected destination. The British plan was to capture Ticonderoga, advance down the Hudson River to crush Washington's forces, and join General Howe's army moving up from New York, thus gaining control in the Hudson River line and severing New England from the other colonies. By destroying the main Continental army and separating and isolating what the British believed to be the most radical and heavily committed region from the Middle and Southern colonies, it was hoped that the rebellion would be quickly terminated.

The major obstacle in the British path was a precarious American naval presence on Lake Champlain by a small group of miscellaneous vessels under the command of General Benedict Arnold. The British, unable to bring their ships by water from the St. Lawrence River, devised a squadron locally, disassembled their ships for transport overland, and then reassembled them. Arnold could not match these tactics as his resources in materials and workers were inferior to those of the opponent.

On October 16, 1776 the British engaged General Arnold's flotilla, which consisted of two schooners, a sloop, four galleys, and eight gondolas.[44] Arnold, taking his position between Valcour Island and the mainland, decided against meeting the attack while at sea. A fair wind had appeared to be of greater benefit to the enemy than to his own miscellaneous force, which he held at anchor. The action, which lasted for two days, was hot and heavy and ended with the destruction or capture of the American vessels. Faced with superiority in ships and gunfire, Arnold's tiny group fought heroically in a battle whose contribution to the American cause was out of all proportion to the numbers involved. "It was," Mahan wrote, "a strife of pigmies for the prize of a continent."[45]

A tactical defeat, the battle was a strategic victory, for it denied the British quick transit of the lake. By keeping the flotilla intact, Arnold forced the British to spend valuable months preparing to overcome this resistance. The delay extended into the late fall and the bad weather forced a postponement of the British thrust toward Fort Ticonderoga and the Hudson River, thus demonstrating the importance of control of an inland waterway.

During this period an American army was able to regroup and prepare to resist the British campaign that resumed in the spring of 1777 under General Burgoyne. The momentous surrender of the British army at Saratoga on October 17, 1777 was but one of the events linked to the American naval presence on the waters of Lake Champlain. That presence prevented the British in late summer 1776 from moving virtually unopposed through the Hudson River Valley, linking up with the main British army in New York, splitting the colonies, and bringing overwhelming strength against Washington's forces. The culminating effect of these disasters may well have extinguished any hope for success among colonists already divided by loyalties and suffering from the hardships of war. Pressure from constituents could have combined with the evident disintegration of morale and the better judgment of delegates to induce the Congress to sue for peace on almost any terms.[46]

So the contribution of Arnold's squadron to the preservation of Continental military fortunes and the continuation of the struggle was vital if not decisive. As an essential factor in leading to Burgoyne's defeat, it contributed to the formation of the

French alliance. French policy under the guiding hand of Count de Vergennes, Minister of Foreign Affairs, aimed at exploiting British weaknesses and restoring France to its former position of power. Uncertain of the colonial commitment and wary of provoking a war with Great Britain over a "family" dispute, Vergennes played a double game. He aided the rebels by allowing their merchant ships and privateers to use French ports, and by surreptitiously extending financial and material aid. When the first American agent, Silas Deane, arrived in Paris in June 1776 he was received by Vergennes, as were his colleagues Arthur Lee and Benjamin Franklin, who joined him later. Together they constituted a Congressional commission. Among their assignments was the procurement of warships. Eventually they became involved in virtually every aspect of maritime activity, including the commissioning of officers and privateers and the disposition of prizes.[47]

Vergennes further aided the colonists by only allowing British warships to inspect French merchantmen for contraband outside French waters, and by denying the right to intercept any trade between France and its possessions. American ships were thus able to pick up illicit cargo in Haiti and Martinique without the hazard of the Atlantic crossing, and units of the French Navy provided protection in those waters.[48] When the colonies declared their independence the French government departed further from its alleged policy of neutrality. Vergennes seriously contemplated war, and was seeking Spanish assistance until he received news of Washington's defeat in Long Island on August 17, 1776. Frantic instructions from the Congress to the American envoys warned of the consequences of a reduction in French aid. But a majority of the delegates refused to countenance an alliance, which, at the time, France would have rejected.[49] Yet French sympathy for the American cause increased, assistance continued, and by summer of 1777 Vergennes contemplated the offer of an alliance but was deterred by Spain's coolness and word of the successful operations of Burgoyne's army. Then, on December 3, 1777, Paris heard of Burgoyne's surrender at Saratoga, an event that created a mixture of elation and consternation in the courts of Europe.

In England the impact of Saratoga prompted the government to offer to repeal the offensive legislation and allow the colonies a degree of autonomy while remaining within the Empire. Without consulting Spain, Vergennes, anxious to prevent a reconciliation, immediately offered official recognition of the young republic and a formal treaty. Representatives of the two nations signed a treaty of "Amity and Commerce" on February 6, 1778 along the lines that had been defined by Congress, and a "conditional and defensive alliance" which the American envoys concluded on their own initiative without instructions. Silas Dean embarked for America with the treaties, and a race ensued between him and a British delegation empowered to negotiate a settlement. Congress quickly gave unanimous approval to both French treaties, and the complexion of the conflict changed immediately from a domestic war to one that openly involved the European powers. The Americans had exploited successfully the centuries old Anglo-French rivalry, and their war of national liberation had expanded to embrace competition for empire and the power balance in Europe and the rest of the world.

Although the treaties did not bring England and France to war immediately, each began preparations for the disposition of its fleet. The French Navy, depleted from the Seven Years' War, had been restored with great efficiency during the intervening years, always with the objective of resuming the contest with England. French ships were newer and superior to those of the British in construction, rigging, and firepower. As the victorious Royal Navy deteriorated, the French Navy expanded under the vigorous leadership of the Duc de Choiseul-Stainville, who became Minister of Marine in 1761. The perennial handicap of manning the vessels was overcome by a systematic recruiting and training program with improved living conditions aboard ship and, for those times, adequate provision for fair treatment. The French fleets, based at Brest in the Channel and Toulon in the Mediterranean, were fit for duty, and could anticipate action in European and West Indian waters if not along the coast of North America.[50]

The Royal Navy, in terms of its potential, had been marking time. No actual mobilization had occurred and warships allo-

cated to the American effort had been utilized to support the
land forces rather than to implement an effective blockade. This
policy of strangling the colonies was not adopted by the British
government until after the surrender at Saratoga when, with
French involvement imminent, it came too late. The limited
mission of the Royal Navy, heretofore confined to the maintenance of communications with the forces in North America and
combating the irritating raiding operations conducted by rebel
warships and privateers, was now expanded to formidable proportions. In addition to insuring supplies and support for the
army in North America and protecting the commercial trade of
England, it had to defend the homeland from invasion, safeguard
West Indian possessions and India, and prevent French aid from
reaching America. This French aid now included troops and
naval cooperation with Washington's army. For the British First
Lord of the Admiralty, the Earl of Sandwich, the prospect of
war with France was "the moment of truth," for England had
no continental allies who would engage France on land.[51]
Plagued by decaying ships, diminished naval stores, and inadequate dockyard facilities for construction and maintenance,
Sandwich could also complain to Parliament in 1778 "that the
navy had lost eighteen thousand of the seamen employed in the
last war by not having America."[52] The opportunity for the
maximum utilization of British sea power to suppress the colonial rebellion had passed. Now the disposition, preservation and
expansion of the Royal Navy became the first priority in a war
of broadened dimensions that threatened part or all of the
empire, as well as the security of a homeland that had not
experienced a successful invasion in more than six hundred
years.

In America the exhilaration growing out of the alliance and
the outbreak of hostilities that soon followed was tempered by
uncertainty as to what military and naval action the French
contemplated. Naval dispositions began with the Brest fleet
moving into the Channel and the Toulon fleet sailing for the West
Indies. The former engaged a British force off Ushant on July
27, 1778 in an indecisive battle that found each side retiring to a
home port for repairs. Writing of this engagement, Richmond

concluded, "There are many 'ifs' in history, but of one of them there can be no dispute. A decisive victory off Ushant [by the British] would have changed the course of the world's history."[53] British destruction of the Brest fleet would have removed the threat of invasion. The French Toulon fleet under Count d'Estaing which had sailed to the West Indies would have been called back to protect French ports, while units of the Royal Navy would have been free to concentrate on d'Estaing's forces and either bottle them up at Brest or Toulon or defeat them at sea. Spain probably would have remained neutral and the American resistance would have collapsed.

As it turned out, the French were able to maintain a fleet in the Channel, one in the Western Hemisphere that cruised from the West Indies as far north as Newport, Rhode Island, and a squadron in India. The Royal Navy simply was not capable of coping with these disparate forces, supporting an army in America, escorting convoys, and maintaining even a partially effective blockade anywhere.[54] When Spain entered the war in 1779, a combined Franco-Spanish fleet swept the Channel and invasion was averted only by chance, luck, and the ineptitude of the enemy.[55] British strategy shifted from its previous offensive orientation to a defensive stance designed for protection and survival rather than conquest. The Spanish intervention in 1779 posed not only a greater danger to the security of England, but it brought a vigorous assault on the stronghold at Gibraltar, a keystone in the Empire's maritime structure. The British, who for three years had been waging a limited war, were now faced with a conflict that would demand their maximum effort and draw on their total resources.

One immediate effect of the Franco-American treaties was an official salute to the newborn ensign. The first return of a salute by a vessel flying the American flag occurred in October 1776 at St. Croix by the somewhat confused Danish garrison of the fort. Then a Continental brigantine, the *Andrew Doria* had its salute returned on November 16, 1776 at St. Eustatius. Subsequently claimed a mistake by the authorities, this act was disavowed by the Dutch government. The privateer *General Mifflin* was accorded a response at Brest in July 1777 by a French admiral whose government never acknowledged the incident.

The opportunity for an official exchange arose in February 1778 at Quiberon Bay where John Paul Jones, commanding the *Ranger*, asked the commander of a French squadron if this courtesy would be observed. An affirmative response led to these eventful salutes being given on February 14 and repeated the following day, although Jones was upset by his firing of thirteen guns and receiving nine in return. The American Navy had secured another symbol of recognition of the new nation in the international community and further evidence that the French government was sympathetic to the American cause.[56]

Meanwhile, in the two years preceding the French entry into the war, the American maritime effort had produced a mixed bag of results. While the year 1776 was studded with successes, including the strategic action on Lake Champlain, not one of the thirteen frigates authorized by Congress in December 1775 was ready for service. By the end of the year a few were close to being prepared for sea. But construction, manning and other delays prevented some from ever being used.[57] The Congress revealed a perceptible shift toward challenging control of the sea rather than relying on a raiding strategy by enacting legislation on November 20, 1776 to provide for the building of "three ships of seventy-four guns each, five frigates of thirty-six guns, an eighteen-gun brig, and a packet boat." This ambitious plan never materialized. Of the four vessels subsequently launched only one ship of the line, the *America*, was finished, and it was given to France as compensation for the loss of one of its ships.[58] The naval program was continually beset by depleted revenues, a rapid depreciation of the Continental paper currency, shipyard deficiencies in workmen and material, and the difficulty of raising crews in competition with the greater appeal of privateering. Consequently, the attempt to provide a more adequate and effective navy foundered during the years 1777 and 1778. Accelerated activity of the Royal Navy in American waters coupled with abortive attempts to employ naval craft in support of land operations aggravated the misfortunes that plagued the American naval effort.

Casting about for ways to employ their tiny forces against the British maritime dominance, the Congress, through its Committee of Foreign Affairs, proposed to the Commissioners in Paris in December 1777 that American frigates be dispatched to India to prey on ocean and coastal trade. Deeming this project impracticable, the commissioners countered with a suggestion that British whaling ships in the southwest Atlantic and the Arctic would be vulnerable targets. Neither of these proposed ventures was undertaken, and American armed vessels confined themselves to operations in North America, the West Indies, and the European coastline.[59]

Still, both Robert Morris and John Paul Jones urged a more aggressive naval strategy, one where the Continental Navy would assault English settlements. Morris favored attacking those in the West Indies while Jones advocated a bolder strike at towns in the British Isles and shipping in home waters. Authorities in London, compelled to divert forces scheduled for the colonies, would thereby relieve pressure on the Americans. Regular commerce raiding, the two men agreed, should be reserved for privateers which could not perform more complex duties.

Jones served on the *Alfred* in Hopkins' fleet and later was given command of the sloop *Providence*. Venturing to the Bahamas, Jones captured a number of prizes and had some narrow escapes from British frigates. Promoted to the rank of captain, he held several other commands until, on June 14, 1777, Congress by resolution gave him command of the 20 gun sloop *Ranger*. Proceeding to France, Jones was soon able to implement his plans for carrying the war to the enemy.

Under the jurisdiction of the American Commissioners in Paris, Jones left Brest on April 10, 1778 and burned a number of ships in the harbor at Whitehaven. On the return voyage the *Ranger* encountered the British man of war *Drake*, which surrendered after a sharp engagement. Many of Jones' ambitious proposals were frustrated by inadequate French support and by discipline problems with his various mixed crews. But in June 1779 he led a squadron into the British seas for what was to be his most notable venture. Hoisting his flag in the 42 gun converted merchantman *Bonhomme Richard*, the Commodore was accompanied by three other vessels: the *Alliance*, a 32 gun frigate under Captain Pierre Landais, *Pallas* of 32 guns, and *Vengeance* of 12 guns.

For some weeks the cruise was routine, relieved only by taking some prizes. Then, on September 23, two English warships were sighted escorting a convoy. Jones, ordering his ships to form in line of battle, headed his flagship for the *Serapis* of 50 guns, the most powerful of the enemy escorts. Unaccountably, Jones' signal was ignored. *Alliance* and *Vengeance* veered off, *Pallas* engaged the 20 gun *Countess of Scarborough*, and *Bonhomme Richard* was left alone to engage the *Serapis*. An exchange of broadsides convinced Jones that musket fire and boarding offered the best opportunity for success, so by adroit maneuvering he managed to bring the two vessels together. At point blank range, the English cannon were more effective in hull destruction, but American marksmanship prevailed topside. Subsequently the *Alliance* joined the action and her broadsides struck both vessels. After two hours of incessant battering, with *Bon Homme Richard* and *Serapis* in desperate straits, the British captain struck his colors and Jones transferred his flag from his sinking ship to the *Serapis*. Meanwhile, the *Pallas* under Captain Thomas Piercy had captured the *Countess of Scarborough*, and the damaged squadron was able to elude searching enemy forces and return to port for repairs. The British convoy, however, reached its destination safely.

Jones never again had an opportunity to raid British water but his reputation as the most illustrious American naval hero of the Revolution endured. Ambitious, headstrong, and egotistical, his abilities, courage, and will overcame odds and provided an example and an inspiration for the colonists and following generations of naval personnel.[60]

The anticipated French military assistance, although no specific agreement had been made, first materialized when the Toulon fleet under Count d'Estaing appeared off the Delaware coast after a leisurely passage that enabled the British army to evacuate Philadelphia and move with the supporting fleet to New York. Washington, deploring this lost opportunity to capture the escaping forces, proceeded with plans for a joint assault at New York. These plans went awry when d'Estaing, fearing that his ships would be grounded on a sand bar, refused to attack.[61] Frustrated in this first attempt to cooperate with the Americans, d'Estaing implemented an alternative plan made with Washington. He sailed for Narragansett Bay to join an American army in an assault on the British position in southern Rhode Island and Newport, and the appearance of an inferior enemy fleet brought preparations for a naval action. But as the two opponents maneuvered for position a storm dispersed the ships and caused heavy damage. Thereupon d'Estaing, in spite of vigorous appeals from the American General John Sullivan, limped off to Boston for repairs.

Deprived of French assistance, the American troops withdrew and recriminations began. General Sullivan issued intemperate charges against the French move, charges which so disturbed many Americans that, anxious to prevent a rupture between the allies, officials made no protest over the incident.[62] Disappointment was keen, however, at what appeared to be a sequence of events illustrating the French lack of enthusiasm in providing military assistance to the desperate Americans. The late arrival of the Toulon fleet, its slow pursuit of the British departure from the Delaware Bay, and its refusal to participate in the New York operation for what seemed to some an inadequate excuse, was now culminated by an apparent desertion of American forces at Newport. It was strange behavior indeed from a professed ally, and the performance of d'Estaing's fleet brought doubts to the minds of many Americans as to what the future would hold. Yet the feeling was so strong that independence could be achieved only with the help of France that recriminations were muted.

After refitting and provisioning, d'Estaing left Boston on November 4, 1778 bound for Martinique. Weather was a significant factor in determining areas of operations, for winter storms on the North Coast of America and the summer hurricane season in the Caribbean posed a constant threat to fleet activity. Further, the alliance with the United Colonies had disavowed any French claims on territory in North America, but had provided for the acquisition of British holdings in the West

Indies. After some minor successes, d'Estaing was ordered to return to Toulon, and en route made an abortive attempt to capture Savannah, Georgia, from the British.[63] He was then replaced by Comte de Guichen, who clashed indecisively with the Royal Navy in the West Indies, while Spain's entry into the war brought little cooperation between the allies in that theater of operations.

In July 1780 de Guichen, ordered back to France, refused the pleas of the Marquis de Lafayette and the French minister in Philadelphia to cooperate with Washington in joint campaigns against the British. Nine months later, on March 22, 1781, Comte de Grasse sailed from Brest for Martinique escorting a convoy of transports that reached its destination after an encounter with a British fleet. Then in June the weather and appeals from Washington and General Comte de Rochambeau, commander of the French troops in America, persuaded de Grasse to join an operation against the British forces in New York or on the Chesapeake. The West Indies remained the most valuable enemy possession and the primary spoil of war sought by the French. But the advent of the hurricane season there made a move to northern waters both desirable and militarily feasible.

The French alliance and the subsequent participation of Spain in the war had not brought the tangible benefits anticipated by many Americans. The impact of these formidable adversaries was felt in London where it created dissention in the government regarding strategy and the allocation of resources. But Britain's troubles were not perceived or appreciated in America, where the enemy appeared stronger than ever, and had launched a massive campaign in the south, reducing American fortunes to a new low. To Americans, the Franco-Spanish efforts seemed to be directed at the periphery of the British military perimeter rather than its main source of strength, namely, the armies in North America. Each of the allies' strategies was influenced, if not determined, by its own war aims. The French had designs on British West Indian islands and the Spanish were determined to regain Gibraltar, objectives only indirectly related to the colonial aim of independence. Success in all or any of these endeavors would help restore the power balance upset by the

Seven Years' War, a disequilibrium the Americans had exploited in gaining allies. But an alteration in the European power structure was not what they were fighting for.

Washington, whose letters in 1780 reveal discouragement and pessimism, took the unusual step on January 15, 1781 of writing directly to Vergennes. "Next to a loan of money," he wrote, "a constant naval superiority on these coasts is the object most interesting." British troops would be compelled to adopt a defensive posture, their sources of supply would be severed, and American forces could assume a "vigorous offensive."[64] His letters to French and American leaders in April, May, and June were filled with complaints about the inability to move effectively against British forces without sea control. On hearing in August of de Grasse's contemplated departure for the Chesapeake, Washington began to plan and prepare for the long-sought collaboration.

The French fleet, composed of twenty-four ships of the line, left Haiti on August 5, 1781 and dropped anchor in the Chesapeake on the 30th preparatory to escorting troops and preventing reinforcements from reaching General Lord Cornwallis and his army in Virginia. Meanwhile, a British fleet had sailed from Antigua for the Chesapeake. Finding no enemy vessels, it proceeded to New York. Reappraising the situation, concern about the army in Virginia prompted the British Admiral Thomas Graves, with nineteen ships, to sail for the Chesapeake.

Arriving on September 5, Graves was surprised to find de Grasse inside, and the latter immediately got underway to fight. The French fleet, allowed to reach the open sea, engaged indecisively. Afer a few days of maneuvering the British fleet broke off and returned to New York. The "victory" at the Battle of the Virginia Capes enabled de Grasse to support the Allied armies in their move to Jamestown by water, and prevented the British troops from receiving aid or from being evacuated from what had become an untenable position. French control of the sea, temporary though it was, provided the essential ingredient for a campaign that culminated in the epochal surrender of Cornwallis' army at Yorktown on September 19, 1781.[65]

The victory at Yorktown restored American faith in the efficacy of French aid, faith that had diminished during 1779 and 1780 when cooperation had eluded the allies.[66] Yet Americans failed to understand the true significance of the surrender, namely, its impact on the British government and people. The shock in England brought on a clamor for peace and a new government, and virtually ended any hope for subduing the colonies.[67] To Washington's dismay, the French fleet departed for the West Indies and suffered a crushing defeat in April 1782 by a British force under Admiral Sir George Rodney at the Battle of the Saints. Writing to Lafayette the month following the Yorktown victory, Washington forecast the "total extirpation" of the British army in the south if de Grasse had remained longer, and reiterated his conviction that "no land force can act decisively unless it is accompanied by a naval superiority."[68] Little did Washington know that never again would he enjoy such an advantage, and that combat operations in America would wind down as a new British government sought peace with its rebellious offspring and concentrated its military effort on the European foes in an attempt to salvage as much as possible from a war that had become too burdensome.

During the final years of the war the Continental Navy declined in strength and made no appreciable impact on the outcome. Most of its efforts were confined to single actions that involved the capture of British merchantmen and transports or encounters with enemy privateers and warships, some marked by brave and noble exploits that brought credit to the service and established a tradition that has endured in the American Navy. Most Continental warships were destroyed by burning alongside the dock or at anchor to avoid capture, or were surrendered when Charleston fell in 1780. Privateering continued to increase as each year more commissions were issued. These armed vessels constituted, with a few exceptions, the major American contribution to the assault on Britain's maritime strength.

It became apparent that victory was at hand when after Yorktown the new British government made secret overtures to the American commissioners in Paris. France saw its dreams of West Indian conquest evaporate when de Grasse's fleet was decimated at the Battle of the Saints,[69] and the relief of the siege at Gibraltar made unlikely the Spanish recovery of this bastion. In England, the King and Parliament grudgingly became reconciled to the loss of what has been called the first British Empire, reconciled in large part because of the exhausted state of the Royal Navy.[70]

The drawn-out conflict produced significant developments in international maritime law: specifically, as to the rights of neutral nations to trade with belligerents. When war first began, the old rule that enemy goods were subject to capture even if carried in the vessel of a neutral country was supplanted in various treaties by the doctrine "free ships make free goods," contraband excepted. Yet this new doctrine was not universally accepted. Britain, in the absence of a treaty declaring otherwise, applied the old rule *Consolato del Mare* that enemy property was subject to confiscation if carried in neutral ships. Trade with belligerents was a profitable enterprise for neutrals since demand for certain products increased in time of war and normal sources were often closed. The question of "free goods" was further complicated by disagreement over the definition of contraband. The American Treaty of Amity and Commerce with France incorporated the principle of "free ships make free goods" and defined items that would be considered contraband, essentially, materials for waging war such as firearms and gunpowder. The English interpreted contraband broadly, often including naval stores and even food, and protests from neutral nations were rejected during the early years of the Revolution. A French decree of July 26, 1778, after her entry into the war, asserted the principle of free ships make free goods and called on the neutral governments to secure British compliance. Britain responded on October 19, 1778 by declaring that "after November 10, neutral vessels and cargoes would be confiscated if they carried enemy property or contraband, including naval stores."[71]

Another controversial issue related to the law of blockade. Merchantmen attempting to enter blockaded ports were, with their cargoes, subject to capture and confiscation. But this conventional practice was confused because no agreement had been reached on what constituted a "legal" or "effective" blockade. A mere declaration that a port had been put in a blockaded status was not sufficient to justify confiscation, at least in the opinion of many governments, especially neutrals. During the war of the American Revolution a number of nations tried to clarify this matter by prescribing the coverage required of blockading vessels. England, consistent with her reliance on sea power, was determined to exploit her control of the sea to the utmost. Interrupting the trade of her enemies, therefore, was an essential part of her strategy. British disregard of the "free ships make free goods" principle, employment of "paper" blockades to justify seizures, and an expanded definition of what constituted contraband, created friction with neutrals, brought on war with the Netherlands, and led to the establishment of the Armed Neutrality.

This organization of neutrals evolved as the British government continued to ignore diplomatic protests over the high-handed activities of the Royal Navy. A complex series of events and negotiations led to a Declaration by Catherine II of Russia on February 28, 1780, which stipulated the rights of neutrals in time of war and invited adherence by other European states, most of whom eventually subscribed to the convention. This compact incorporated much of the "Plan of 1776" formulated by the Congress and included in the Treaty of Amity and Commerce with France. It constituted a multilateral approach to a codification of the rights of neutrals at sea during war in international law.

Often referred to disparagingly as the "Armed Nullity," a term applied by Catherine herself because it employed no military force to make its terms effective, this declaration and concert of nations finally induced the British government to modify its policies and conform more closely to the evolutionary principles of the law of the sea. Some contend that there was no such thing as international law because it had no legislative body to give it legitimacy and no specific enforcement agency. But rules governing the conduct of nations in their relations with each other have existed. Somewhat in the manner of the English common law, they developed over the centuries and have affected the destinies of nations and peoples. Parenthetically, it should be noted that the United States has gone to war on three occasions ostensibly over a violation of its neutral rights, namely, the Quasi-War with France, the War of 1812, and World War I. Elusive though the concept of freedom of the seas may be, the Armed Neutrality served to coerce the British government into conceding to the weaker maritime powers a set of rules that, often honored in the breach, had a direct impact on the American Navy and the nation.[72] The Congress adopted, by resolutions, the principles contained in the Declaration and directed that the Board of Admiralty issue instructions to captains of "armed vessels commanded by the United States" to observe them. Yet the United States never formally adhered to the convention of the Armed Neutrality, in large part because Catherine did not want to imply recognition of American independence.[73]

Naval warfare during the war of the American Revolution was not drastically altered by technological innovation. Perhaps the most significant development was the sheathing of ship's bottoms with copper, a practice that, after some bureaucratic resistance, became widespread in the Royal Navy during the years 1778 to 1781. The fouling of ship's bottoms by barnacles and parasites plagued seafarers since time immemorial, interfering with the seaworthiness of the vessel and its maneuverability. Removal of these growths required beaching [careening] or drydocking twice a year to scrape off the offending organisms and repair damage done to the hull. The copper sheathing acted as a preservative and allowed vessels to remain in maximum service efficiency for a much longer period. Unencumbered by the accumulation of foreign substances on the bottom that impeded progress, the ship's speed was increased, it was easier to handle, and it was more often available for service. Introduced only sporadically in the French Navy, copper sheathing may have contributed in some degree to the survivability of the Royal Navy during the prolonged conflict.[74]

Conventional firepower was enhanced by the introduction of the carronade. A short barreled, low velocity, heavy shot gun, it was particularly effective at short range. First introduced in the British Navy, it became popular with the French service because of its usefulness against rigging and personnel topside. Eventually the carronade was rendered obsolete by improvements in gunfire that made it impossible for ships to engage at the effective close distance.[75]

Experiences of the war were not entirely lost on those in the American government who foresaw the need for sea power in the survival of the new nation and the fulfillment of its destiny. Despite the demise of the first American Navy after independence was won, there were many who planned for and looked forward to a rebirth of the maritime arm that had elevated the mother country to greatness, sustained the colonies, and contributed so much to the creation of another world power.[76]

NOTES

1. The fullest account is Neil R. Stout, *The Royal Navy in America, A Study of Enforcement of British Colonial Policy in the Era of the American Revolution 1760–1775* (Annapolis, 1973), which emphasizes the role of the Royal Navy's enforcement of laws in bringing on the Revolution. For the colonists' reaction, see George Louis Beer, *British Colonial Policy, 1754–1765* (New York, 1907), 288–294; David S. Lovejoy, *Rhode Island Politics and the American Revolution, 1760–1776* (Providence, RI, 1958), 36; Charles M. Andrews, *The Colonial Period of American History: England's Commercial and Colonial Policy* (4 vols, New Haven, 1934–1938), IV, 422; Jesse Lemisch, "Jack Tar in the Streets: Merchant Seamen in the Politics of Revolutionary America," *William and Mary Quarterly*, Third Series, XXV (July 1968), 371–395. Although the latter may exaggerate the amount of discontent aroused by impressment and treatment aboard ship, one British admiral observed that vessels were "manned by violence and maintained by cruelty." Quoted in J. C. Beaglehole, *The Life of Captain James Cook* (Stanford, 1974), 15. Stout concludes that "impressment did not become a great issue of the American Revolution." Neil R. Stout, "Manning the Royal Navy in North America, 1763–1775," *The American Neptune*, XXIII (July 1963), 184.

2. Charles Oscar Paullin, *Paullin's History of Naval Administration, 1775–1911: A Collection of Articles from the Naval Institute Proceedings* (Annapolis, 1968), 57; William Bell Clark, "American Naval Policy, 1775–1776," *The American Neptune*, I (1941), 27. Evidently the proposal was defeated by "moderates." *Ibid.*

3. William Bell Clark, *George Washington's Navy: Being an Account of His Excellency's Fleet in New England Waters* (Baton Rouge, 1960); Dudley

W. Knox, *The Naval Genius of George Washington* (Boston, 1932), 8–9; Gardner W. Allen, *A Naval History of the American Revolution* (2 vols, Boston, 1913), I, 59–89. The Congress subsequently approved Washington's actions on 25 November 1775. William Bell Clark and William James Morgan, eds., *Naval Documents of the American Revolution* (9 vols, Washington, 1964–1986), II, 1131–1133.

4. Allen, *Naval History of the American Revolution*, I, 86–89. The officers and crew of "Washington's Navy" received a share of the profits from the capture of non-military cargo. William J. Morgan, *Captains to the Northward: The New England Captains in the Continental Navy* (Barre, MA, 1959), 7. Prizes taken are listed in Clark, *George Washington's Navy*, 229–236.

5. Congress resolved on 18 July 1775 "That each colony, at their own expense, make such provisions by armed vessels, or otherwise, as their respective assemblies, conventions, or committees of safety shall judge expedient and suitable to their circumstances and situation for the protection of their harbours and navigation on their sea coasts, against all unlawful invasions, attacks, and depredations from cutters and ships of war." Clark and Morgan, *Naval Documents of the American Revolution*, I, 916. Brief accounts of the colonial (state) committees or councils of safety may be found in Allan Nevins, *The American States During and After the Revolution, 1775–1789* (New York, 1924); and Agnes Hunt, *The Provincial Committees of Safety of the American Revolution* (reprint, New York, 1968). The contention that New Jersey and Delaware were the only states without their own navies is challenged by Robert L. Scheina, "A Matter of Definition: A New Jersey Navy, 1777–1783," *The American Neptune*, XXXIX (July 1979), 209–218.

6. Morgan contends that Washington "acted under the general authority vested in him as Commander in Chief of the Army. He sought no further approval from Congress for his action." *Captains to the Northward*, 11. Washington's concern over the legality of his actions is mentioned in Clark, "American Naval Policy, 1775–1776," 30. One writer labels this sailing the "Birth of the American Navy." Vincent J. Dowell, Jr., "The Birth of the American Navy," *U.S. Naval Institute Proceedings*, 81 (November 1955), 1251–1257.

7. Allen, *Naval History of the Revolution*, I, 23. The Rhode Island resolution is printed in Clark and Morgan, *Naval Documents of the American Revolution*, I, 1236; the Congressional resolution of 5 October is printed in *ibid.* II, 307–309; that of 30 October in *ibid.* II, 647.

8. Information on these early committees may be found in Allen, *Naval History of the Revolution*, I, 22–23; *Paullin's History of Naval Administration*, 5–6; Clark, "American Naval Policy 1775–1776," 32–34; Edmund Cody Burnett, *The Continental Congress* (New York, 1941), 119–120. There is some confusion about the composition of the first committee, for, as John Adams later wrote: "The secretary has omitted to insert the names of the committee on the journals . . ." Quoted in Clark and Morgan, *Naval Documents of the American Revolution*, II, 308, footnote 2.

9. The "Rules" are printed in *ibid.*, 1174–1182; and in Allen, *Naval History of the American Revolution,* II, Appendix II, 686–695. For their source see Frederic H. Hayes, "John Adams and American Sea Power," *The American Neptune,* XXV (1965), 36, especially footnote 8.

10. These resolutions of 25 November 1775 are printed in Clark and Morgan, *Naval Documents of the American Revolution,* II, 1131–1133. The circumstances are recounted in Clark, "American Naval Policy, 1775–1776," 34–37.

11. The appointment and activities of the Naval Committee are described in *ibid.*, 32–37; *Paullin's History of Naval Administration,* 5–8; Allen, *Naval History of the American Revolution,* I, 22–31. The latter maintains that Hopkins' appointment was not intended to be the equivalent of Washington's in that Hopkins only had command of the squadron. *Ibid.*, 30. The orders issued to Hopkins were "magnificently unrealistic." Sidney G. Morse, "The Fleet," *The American Neptune,* V (April 1945), 177.

12. Burnett, *The Continental Congress,* 60–102; Lloyd Milton Short, *The Development of National Administrative Organization in the United States* (Baltimore, 1923), 36–38; Higginbotham, *The War of American Independence,* 93–94.

13. Clark and Morgan, *Naval Documents of the American Revolution,* III, 90; *Paullin's History of Naval Administration,* 8–9; Allen, *Naval History of the American Revolution,* I, 25–26. For details on the vessels authorized, see Marion V. Brewington, "The Designs of Our First Frigates," *The American Neptune,* VIII (1948), 11–25. William P. Bass, "Who Did Design the First U.S. Frigates?," *Naval History,* V (Summer 1991), 49–54, explores the controversy using contemporary documents.

14. The resolution of August 5 is printed in Clark and Morgan, *Naval Documents of the American Revolution,* VI, 63. This action was directed against Hopkins, not Washington, according to Clark, *George Washington's Navy,* 174. For the "board" of five members, see *Paullin's History of Naval Administration,* 9.

15. *Ibid,* 13–20; Charles O. Paullin, ed., *Out Letters of the Continental Marine Committee and Board of Admiralty* (2 vols, New York, 1914), I, xxvi–xxvii.

16. For the appointment, composition, and work of the Board of Admiralty see Allen, *Naval History of the American Revolution,* I, 35–36; *Paullin's History of Naval Administration,* 31–38.

17. The disintegration of the Continental Navy and its administrative structure is covered in *ibid.*, 44–53; and Allen, *Naval History of the American Revolution,* I, 36–37, II, 615–616. One biographer calls Robert Morris "Father of the Fleet." Eleanor Young, *Forgotten Patriot: Robert Morris* (New York, 1950). Title of the chapter covering Morris' activities as Agent of Marine, 109–117. This is a popular and somewhat superficial account. Congress established a Board of War and Ordnance on June 12, 1776 to deal with army administration. See Kenneth Schaffel, "The American Board of War, 1776–1781," *Military Affairs,* 50 (October 1986), 185–189.

18. The Morison quotation is from Samuel Eliot Morison, *John Paul Jones: A Sailor's Biography* (paperback, New York, 1964), 34. Allen claims that "By this vote [of October 30, 1775] Congress was fully committed to the policy of maintaining a naval armament." *Naval History of the American Revolution,* I, 23. The October 5, 1775 resolution "was the first naval legislation enacted by Congress and, as such, is a truly significant event in the genesis of American naval power." Clark and Morgan, *Naval Documents of the American Revolution,* II, 2.

19. Naval Committee to Commodore Esek Hopkins, January 5, 1776, *ibid.,* III, 637–638; Allen, *Naval History of the American Revolution,* I, 90–105, 118; William M. Fowler, Jr., "Esek Hopkins: Commander-in-Chief of the Continental Navy," in James C. Bradford, ed., *Command Under Sail: Makers of the American Naval Tradition, 1775–1850* (Annapolis, 1985), 3–17. Allen quotes extensively from participant accounts.

20. Clark and Morgan, *Naval Documents of the American Revolution,* IV, 477–480.

21. Edgar S. Maclay, *A History of American Privateers* (New York, 1899), 4–7; Howard M. Chapin, *Privateer Ships and Sailors, The First Century of American Colonial Privateering, 1625–1725* (Toulon, 1926); Chapin, *Privateering in King George's War, 1739–1748* (Providence, 1928).

22. Clark and Morgan, *Naval Documents of the American Revolution,* II, 1131–1133.

23. "A privateer may be described as an armed vessel privately owned, controlled and officered, and commissioned by a belligerent State to commit hostile acts against enemy ships." Charles Cheney Hyde, *International Law Chiefly as Interpreted and Applied by the United States* (3 vols, 2nd ed., Boston, 1951), III, 1914.

24. Clark and Morgan, *Naval Documents of the American Revolution,* II, 1131–1133.

25. *Ibid,* IV, 648–651; Allen, *Naval History of the American Revolution,* II, Appendix III, 695–698. The captain of the vessel was required to deliver a bond of $5,000 for a ship of less than 100 tons and a bond of $10,000 if the displacement was greater. The bond was raised to $20,000 in 1780.

26. Sidney G. Morse, "State or Continental Privateers?", *American Historical Review,* LII (October 1946), 68–73, concludes that after the Congressional resolutions of April 1776 there were few states commissioned privateers. But see William James Morgan, "American Privateering in America's War for Independence, 1775–1783," *The American Neptune,* XXXVI (April 1976), 79–87.

27. Allen, *Naval History of the American Revolution,* I, 42–43. A sharp distinction between a privateer and a "letter of marque" is drawn in Robert Greenhalgh Albion and Jennie Barnes Pope, *Sea Lanes in Wartime: The American Experience, 1775–1942,* (New York, 1942), 24–25.

28. Maclay, *A History of American Privateers,* 506; Allen, *Naval History of the American Revolution,* I, 46–47.

29. *Ibid.*, 51–52. "It was in Caribbean rather than European waters that American privateers posed a serious threat to British commerce." Alan G. Jamieson, "American Privateering in the Leeward Islands, 1776–1778," *The American Neptune*, XLIII (January 1983), 20.

30. Maclay, *A History of American Privateers*, xi.

31. Carroll Storrs Alden and Ralph Earle, *Makers of Naval Tradition* (Boston, 1925), 11. The role of commerce raiding as a contribution to the American naval effort is also denigrated in Harold and Margaret Sprout, *The Rise of American Naval Power, 1776–1918* (Princeton, 1942), 11. The reputation of the land militia has been somewhat restored after years of suffering under the onslaught of Emory Upton's *The Military Policy of the United States* (Washington, 1904). See Russell F. Weigley, *History of the United States Army* (New York, 1967), 44–73; and some good words are said for the Continental Army in Higginbotham, *The War of American Independence*, 412–414.

32. Details on privateering during the War of the American Revolution may be found in Maclay, *A History of American Privateers;* Allen, *Naval History of the American Revolution,* and his *Massachusetts Privateers of the Revolution* (Boston, 1927). William Bell Clark, *Ben Franklin's Privateers: A Naval Epic of the American Revolution,* (Baton Rouge, 1956), is more specialized and stresses that the three vessels commissioned by Franklin were most effective in preying on the coastal trade in the waters around the British Isles (173), although Franklin's motive was to secure prisoners to be exchanged for Americans (v). A popular account is Donald Barr Chidsey, *The American Privateers* (New York, 1962). Privateers commissioned in French ports were manned by heterogeneous crews of many nationalities, often with little or no experience at sea, and these privateers usually flew the French flag. Allen, *Naval History of the American Revolution,* II, 598–599. Discipline and enemy vessels were constant problems.

33. *Ibid.*, I, 285–286; Bemis, *The Diplomacy of the American Revolution,* 53–55.

34. Mahan, *The Influence of Seapower Upon History,* 330–541; and his *Major Operations of the Navies in the War of American Independence* (Boston, 1913; reprint, New York, 1969). John A. Tilley, *The British Navy and the American Revolution* (Columbia, SC, 1987), stresses naval commanders and North American actions.

35. An admirable summation of the American strategy during the Revolution is Russell F. Weigley, *The American Way of War: A History of United States Military Strategy and Policy* (New York, 1973), 3–39. A fuller recent account is Higginbotham, *The War of American Independence.*

36. Opinions vary on the efficacy of a blockade of the colonies. Higginbotham contends that it would have been ineffectual. *Ibid.*, 150. Thinking otherwise is Piers Mackesy, *The War for America, 1775–1783* (Cambridge, MA, 1964), 97–102.

37. Wheeden, *Economic and Social History of New England,* II, 764–765;

Lawrence H. Gipson, *The British Empire Before the American Revolution: The Triumphant Empire, 1763–1766* (New York, 1956), 17; Marcus, *A Naval History of England: The Formative Centuries,* 346. Mackesy contends that there was not a shortage of "great masts" until 1780, although "made-masts" came in short supply in 1778 following the Battle of Ushant due to the French tactic of concentrating fire on the masts and rigging. *The War for America,* 168–169. Marcus asserts that "It was the timber shortage that was primarily responsible for the long delay in fitting out squadrons against the Brest and Toulon fleets when France entered the war in 1778." *A Naval History of England: The Formative Centuries,* 416.

38. *Ibid.,* 414.

39. *Ibid.,* 372, 416. "Of all the branches of naval administration, it was recruiting which bore with deadliest effect on strategy." Mackesy, *The War for America,* 177. "The chief limitations affecting the performance of the early navies were supply and health. It was impossible to provide sufficient stores or to keep men fit for more than a few weeks at a time. Not until the end of the eighteenth century could large ships remain at sea for prolonged periods." Graham, *The Politics of Naval Supremacy,* 13, footnote 2. The multifarious problems that plagued the Royal Navy are well portrayed in Mackesy, *The War for America,* 162–179. Shipboard medical care is described in Maurice Bear Gordon, "Naval and Maritime Medicine During the Revolution," in Clark and Morgan, *Naval Documents of the American Revolution,* VI, Appendix A, 1483–1489; and Maurice Bear Gordon, *Naval and Maritime Medicine During the American Revolution* (Ventnor, NJ, 1978).

40. The "coercive and . . . conciliatory character" of the campaign are deemed contradictory by Higginbotham, *The War of American Independence,* 149.

41. Mackesy includes these and other factors in accounting for the failure. *The War for America,* 74 ff. For a full account of Howe's efforts, see Ira D. Gruber, "Richard Lord Howe, Admiral as Peacemaker," in George Athan Billias, ed., *George Washington's Opponents: British Generals and Admirals in the American Revolution* (New York, 1969), 233—259. The author concludes that the plan incorporating "a show of strength, a limited use of force, and repeated overtures to the colonists . . . might have succeeded had not Washington spoiled the Hessians' Christmas at Trenton." *Ibid.,* 252.

42. The resolution was introduced by Richard Henry Lee who had written on June 2, 1776, "It is not choice then but necessity that calls for Independence, as the only means by which foreign Alliance can be obtained." Lee to Landon Carter, in Edmund Cody Burnett, ed., *Letters of Members of the Continental Congress* (8 vols, Washington, 1921–1938), I, 463.

43. Washington to the President of Congress, July 25, 1777, Clark and Morgan, *Naval Documents of the American Revolution,* IX, 336. Clark emphasizes Washington's gradual awareness of the role of sea power. *George Washington's Navy,* 243, footnote 2. For a summary appraisal see Knox, *The Naval Genius of George Washington,* 123–128.

44. Mahan, *Major Operations of the Navies in the War of American Independence*, 17. There is some dispute over the relative worth in combat of galleys and gondolas. Arnold favored the former, i.e., row galleys, probably in part because they could be maneuvered more easily in the Lake and the confining waters around Valcour Island where he determined to make his stand. The expense and difficulty of constructing larger warships were controlling factors. Arnold also complained about his "wretched motley crew." Letter to Major General Horatio Gates, 18 September 1776, in Clark and Morgan, *Naval Documents of the American Revolution*, VI, 884.

45. Mahan, *Major Operations of the Navies in the War of American Independence*, 18. The Lake Champlain operation and its significance are described and analysed in *ibid.*, 6–28; and Allen, *Naval History of the American Revolution*, I, 161–179. Mahan refers to the action perceptively in his *Naval Strategy, Compared and Contrasted with the Principles and Practices of Military Operations on Land* (Boston, 1911), 95. One writer notes that "the British naval victory had been complete, but the sheer construction of the American fleet had long delayed Carleton's advance." Willard W. Wallace, "Benedict Arnold: Traitorous Patriot," in George Athan Billias, ed., *George Washington's Generals* (New York, 1964), 177.

46. The "causal connection" between the naval situation on Lake Champlain and the surrender of Burgoyne is emphasized in Allen, *Naval History of the American Revolution*, I, 179; Mahan, *Major Operations of the Navies in the War of American Independence*, 25; Mahan, *Naval Strategy*, 95. See also Higginbotham, *The War of American Independence*, 162; Mackesy, *The War for America*, 94–96; and Paul H. Smith, "Sir Guy Carleton: Soldier Statesman," in Billias, ed., *George Washington's Opponents*, 124–125, 127.

47. The initial reception and activities of these envoys are described in Bemis, *Diplomacy of the American Revolution*, 29–40. Naval affairs functions in Paris are treated in Clark, *Ben Franklin's Privateers;* Charles O. Paullin, *The Navy of the American Revolution; Its Administration, Its Policy and Its Achievements* (Cleveland, 1906), chapter IX; Paullin, *Diplomatic Negotiations of American Naval Officers, 1778–1888* (Reprint, Gloucester, MA, 1967), 11–29. The exploits of John Paul Jones on land and sea are vividly and authoritatively portrayed in Morison, *John Paul Jones*, previously cited.

48. Bemis, *Diplomacy of the American Revolution*, 38–39. These actions were taken in May and June 1776. The French Navy was directed to protect American vessels from the British Navy if requested to do so. Louis XVI to Count Louis Charles Du Chaffault, 12 May 1776, Clark and Morgan, *Naval Documents of the American Revolution*, IV, 1120–1122.

49. Malbone W. Graham, *American Diplomacy in the International Community* (Baltimore, 1948), 9–24.

50. Mahan, *The Influence of Sea Power Upon History*, 331–336; Lewis, *The History of the British Navy*, 156–160; Christopher Lloyd, "Armed Forces and the Art of War: Navies," in A. Goodwin, ed., *The American and French*

Revolutions, 1763–93 (Cambridge, 1965), 183–190; Jenkins, *A History of the French Navy*, 142–147.

51. Mackesy, *The War for America*, 163.

52. Quoted in Mahan, *The Influence of Sea Power Upon History*, 344. Sandwich's "defensive and supine" strategy is criticized in Willcox, "Arbuthnot, Gambier, and Graves," 262.

53. Richmond, *Statesmen and Sea Power*, 150.

54. *Ibid.*, 147; Mackesy, *The War for America*, 194; Lewis, *The History of the British Navy*, 160.

55. A. T. Patterson, *The Other Armada: The Franco-Spanish Attempt to Invade Britain in 1779* (Manchester, 1960). Jenkins places most of the blame for the failure on "the French planners and administrators." *A History of the French Navy*, 161.

56. Allen, *Naval History of the American Revolution*, I, 159, 280–281, 338–340; Bemis, *Diplomacy of the American Revolution*, 122–123; Morison, *John Paul Jones*, 127–129; Barbara W. Tuchman, *The First Salute* (New York, 1988).

57. Allen, *Naval History of the American Revolution*, I, 155 ff., 182–185. The definitive account of early American men-of-war is Howard I. Chapelle, *The History of the American Sailing Navy: The Ships and Their Development* (New York, 1949). Supplementing Chapelle in certain categories are Brian Lavery, *The Ship of the Line* (2 vols, Annapolis, 1984); and Jean Boudriot, *The Seventy-Four-Gun Ship* (4 vols, Annapolis, 1987–1989). A brief illustrated description is in Naval History Division, *Dictionary of American Naval Fighting Ships* (8 vols, Washington, 1959–1991), IV, Appendix V, 610–619. These volumes contain information on each ship commissioned, including duty assignments, and descriptive appendices.

58. Allen, *Naval History of the American Revolution*, I, 183–184.

59. *Ibid.*, 251–252; Charles O. Paullin, *American Voyages to the Orient, 1690–1865: An Account of Merchant and Naval Activities in China, Japan, and the Various Pacific Islands* (Annapolis, 1971), 6–7.

60. The "Battle off Flamborough Head" is detailed in Morison, *John Paul Jones*, 220–242; and Allen, *Naval History of the American Revolution*, II, 457–476; John Evangelist Walsh, *Night on Fire: The First Complete Account of John Paul Jones's Greatest Battle* (New York, 1978).

61. Mahan is critical of d'Estaing's conduct of the French fleet from the late arrival at the Delaware through the abortive New York episode. *Major Operations of the Navies in the War of American Independence*, 62–68.

62. William C. Stinchcombe, *The American Revolution and the French Alliance* (Syracuse, 1969), 48–61. Jenkins contends that d'Estaing's "failure to take Newport was largely due to the tardy arrival of the United States militia, who were to co-operate." *A History of the French Navy*, 153, footnote 1. Higginbotham admits that "one may cavil at his [d'Estaing's] precipitous withdrawal." *The War of American Independence*, 149. A full account is Paul F. Deardon, *The Rhode Island Campaign of 1778: Inauspicious Dawn of*

Alliance (Providence, 1980). A contemporary account of friction between French and American sailors ashore in Boston and Charleston is printed in Henry Steele Commager and Richard B. Morris, eds., *The Spirit of Seventy-Six: The Story of the American Revolution as Told by Participants* (2 vols, Indianapolis, 1958), II, 720–721.

63. Mahan, stressing that "in war the proper main objective is the enemy's navy," wrote, "There is something pitiful in seeing the efforts of a great naval force, with the enemy's fleet within its reach, directed towards unimportant land stations, as was the case with the French fleet under d'Estaing in the West Indies during 1778 and 1779." *Naval Strategy*, 199.

64. Quoted in Allen, *Naval History of the American Revolution*, II, 547. Excerpts from Washington's correspondence are quoted in Mahan, *The Influence of Sea Power Upon History*, 398–399.

65. The naval side of the operation that culminated with the surrender at Yorktown is described in Knox, *The Naval Genius of George Washington*, 87–116; Mahan, *Major Operations of the Navies in the War of American Independence*, 175–184; Allen, *Naval History of the American Revolution*, II, 571–575; William J. Morgan, "The Pivot Upon Which Everything Turned: French Naval Superiority That Insured Victory at Yorktown," *The Ironworker*, 22 (Spring 1958), 1–9. A perceptive analysis of the British failure at army-navy cooperation is William B. Willcox, "The British Road to Yorktown: A Study in Divided Command," *American Historical Review*, LII (October 1946), 1–35. John O. Sands, *Yorktown's Captive Fleet* (Charlottesville, VA, 1983), combines conventional research with underwater archeology.

66. Stinchcombe, *The American Revolution and the French Alliance*, 183.

67. Richard B. Morris, *The Peacemakers: The Great Powers and American Independence* (New York, 1965), 251–252.

68. Quoted in Allen, *Naval History of the American Revolution*, II, 580. Washington concluded: "A constant naval superiority would terminate the war speedily; without it I do not know that it will ever be terminated honorably." *Ibid.*

69. On news of this defeat the French government was not discouraged. But subsequently it could not recover from the loss and was influenced accordingly in its accommodation for peace. Morris, *The Peacemakers*, 276, 390; Jenkins, *A History of the French Navy*, 198.

70. Morris, *The Peacemakers*, 421.

71. Bemis, *Diplomacy of the American Revolution*, 149.

72. *Ibid.*, 149–163; Isabel de Madariaga, *Britain, Russia and the Armed Neutrality of 1780: Sir James Harris's Mission to St. Petersburg During the American Revolution* (New Haven, 1962). The latter maintains that the Armed Neutrality was more effective than do some authorities. Marcus contends that Britain bowed to the demand to recognize the "free ships free goods" doctrine because she wanted to continue receiving timber and naval stores from the Baltic states and realized that the formidable naval power of the coalition could

be employed against British commerce and privateers. *A Naval History of England: The Formative Centuries,* 430–431.

73. Allen, *Naval History of the American Revolution,* II, 542–543.

74. Maurer Maurer, "Coppered Bottoms for the Royal Navy: A Factor in the Maritime War of 1778–1783," *Military Affairs,* XIV (1950), 67–61; A. L. Cross, "On Coppering Ship's Bottoms," *American Historical Review,* XXXIII (1927–1928), 79–81; R. J. B. Knight, "The Introduction of Copper Sheathing, 1779–1786," *Mariner's Mirror,* 59 (1973), 299–309.

75. Spencer C. Tucker, "The Carronade," *U.S. Naval Institute Proceedings,* 99 (August 1973), 65–70; Marion V. Brewington, "American Naval Guns, 1775–1785," *The American Neptune,* III (January 1943), 11–18; III (April 1943), 148–158.

76. The indispensable source for material on the American Navy during the revolution is Clark and Morgan, *Naval Documents of the American Revolution.* This impressive collection of primary sources pertaining to maritime activities during the Revolution includes materials from American and European contemporary printed and archival sources. Profusely illustrated, each volume contains a full bibliography of secondary writings and a detailed index. A "must" for any scholar of the period or the "buff" intrigued by the exploits of the sailing navy or the early history of the country. For historiography of the conflict see David Syrett, "American and British Naval Historians and the American Revolutionary War, 1875–1980," *The American Neptune,* XLII (July 1982), 179–192. Syrett deplores the disproportionate amount of writing on the land campaigns in what was primarily a maritime war. For assessments of various aspects of the role of sea power, see Naval History Division, *Maritime Dimensions of the American Revolution* (Washington, 1977), with articles by Frank C. Mevers, David Syrett, William James Morgan, Raymond G. O'Connor, and Edwin B. Hooper. The British perspective is ably presented in David Syrett, *The Royal Navy in American Waters, 1775–1783* (Brookfield, VT 1989). A complementary work is Jonathan Dull, *The French Navy and the American Revolution: A Study of Arms and Diplomacy, 1774–1787* (Princeton, 1975).

Chapter 3
Formulating a Naval Policy, 1783–1801

The virtual elimination of the army was more than matched by the demise of the Continental Navy as the new nation strove to cope with the problems of independence and the euphoria of victory. "Congress itself," as one historian wrote, "collapsed for a time at the end of the war."[1] The absence of armed conflict and the heavy weight of a sizable debt served to divert Congress from making provision for defense against external threats or internal enemies. The loose-knit Articles of Confederation, ratified in 1781, reflected an inherent fear of centralized control and an aversion to a strong national government. Having won their freedom from one government the states were loath to accept another. An inbred suspicion of peacetime military forces and a dispute over the authority of Congress to create an army and navy further discouraged efforts in that direction.[2] Only when leading citizens began to perceive that the conduct of domestic and foreign affairs demanded greater unity and direction and the exercise of more powers than the Articles permitted was momentum generated to form a national government.

American overseas commerce, previously the lifeblood of the colonies, revealed weaknesses stemming from independence. No longer enjoying the privileges of empire preference or the protection of the Royal Navy, American shipping was denied access to certain ports and faced with increased duties at others. Venturing into the Mediterranean to revive old markets and seek new ones, merchantmen suffered the ravages of the Barbary corsairs. American trade with Mediterranean ports had thrived until the Revolution, when it was disrupted by the British Royal Navy and privateers. After independence this trade resumed, stimulated by the curtailment of trade with the former customary ports of the West Indies and England. Barbary raiders had preyed on European vessels for centuries, a practice halted periodically by treaties involving the payment of money and naval stores to the Barbary rulers. Joint or even unilateral military action by the major maritime powers against the common enemy was avoided because of the trouble and expense involved, while the damage to a rival's trade, whether in peace or war, was deemed a justification for tolerating the outrage. Not content with capturing the ship and cargo, these predators often enslaved or held for ransom passengers and members of the crew.[3]

The new nation, under the Articles, had neither a navy to furnish protection nor the funds to purchase immunity for American lives and property. Yet some prominent individuals readily discerned the indispensability of naval force. Washington, in his "Sentiments on a Peace Establishment," advocated "building and equipping a Navy, without which, in case of war we could neither protect our Commerce, nor yield that Assistance to each other, which, on such an extent of Sea-Coast, our mutual safety would require," and he stressed the need for control of the Great Lakes.[4] Thomas Jefferson, as governor of Virginia during the Revolution, became aware of the significance of sea power and deplored the inability of the Commonwealth Navy and the Continental Navy to prevent the interruption of commerce.[5] Although he disparaged the army as a defense against aggression, Jefferson thought a small navy would be effective against whatever portion of a European fleet could be sent across the Atlantic. Further, he noted, "a naval force can never endanger our liberties, nor occasion bloodshed; a land force would do both."[6]

On the diplomatic scene, Jefferson and John Adams as ministers to France and Great Britain, respectively, witnessed at first hand the weakness of their diplomatic efforts as they sought to promote American interests among the nations of Europe, whose monarchial governments were less than sympathetic.

The precarious strategic condition of the new republic was apparent. Cordoned on the north by British Canada, bordered on the west by forts the erstwhile enemy refused to evacuate, it faced Spain on the west and south, which viewed the upstart republic with suspicion and prohibited navigation of the Mississippi. The nation was further plagued by pirates in the Caribbean who attacked American vessels with impunity. Some of the Founding Fathers, steeped in history and tempered by experience, became convinced that independence would not long endure unless certain shortcomings of the Confederation, especially the protection and promotion of vital interests, were resolved.[7]

Consistent with its weak position, the new government found it advantageous to argue for the rights of neutrals in time of war. The Congressional "Treaty Plan of 1784" specified items to be incorporated in treaties: a definition of contraband, the provision of "free ships free goods," contraband excepted, and the stipulation of "effective" blockade.[8] The prospect of another European war caused apprehension among American merchants, and while the Articles authorized Congress to establish a navy, both the funds and the necessary votes were lacking. When during 1785–1786 the Secretary for Foreign Affairs, John Jay, posed the alternatives of relinquishing the carrying trade to vessels of other nations or taking steps to become a "maritime Power," sectional differences prevented a resolution of the question.[9] The failure of Congress to approve the Jay-Gardoqui treaty of 1786, by which Spain would have conceded navigation of the Mississippi in exchange for commercial concessions, revealed to other nations a domestic cleavage and further diminished confidence in the Confederation. The impotence of the government at home and abroad was apparent, and James Madison complained in 1785 that "Our trade was never more compleatly monopolized by Great Britain when it was under the direction of the British Parliament than it is at this moment." Currency and credit were at a low ebb, sources for revenue were minimal, and respect for the United States steadily declined.

Growing support for trade and shipping in American bottoms provided an impetus for a stronger government, one that would enact navigation laws and maintain a military organization to enforce its rights and interests.[10] The Articles had authorized the Congress "to build and equip a navy," and during the Constitutional Convention of 1787 plans were submitted for a department of Admiralty and for the president to "be Commander in chief of the Land Forces of U.S. [sic] and Admiral of their [sic] Navy."[11] The provision that emerged in the Constitution authorizing Congress "to provide and maintain a navy" was the subject of much discussion during the Convention. The controversy surfaced in the states during the debates over ratification, where opinion reflected sectional and political lines. New England and the middle Atlantic states generally supported the Constitution, which provided for a stronger central government and the creation of a navy. Southern and western elements tended to reject both. Although "nationalists" urged adoption of the document on many grounds, a key argument was the need for a more effective military posture to defend the country and implement policies abroad. The "states rights" groups contended that a navy would benefit only the north, would be too expensive, would serve as an instrument for imperialism, and would be unnecessary for defense since 3,000 miles of ocean was a sufficient barrier against aggression.

Writing for the New York constituency in support of the Constitution, Alexander Hamilton, James Madison, and John Jay expounded in "The Federalist Papers" on the benefits of a navy. Hamilton wrote of "a navy which, if it could not vie with those of the great maritime powers, would at least be of respectable weight if thrown into the scale of either of two contending parties," and "enable us to bargain with great advantage for commercial privileges." Further, added Hamilton, "we may hope, ere long, to become the arbiter of Europe in America, and to be able to incline the balance of European competitions in this part of the world as our interest may dictate." As for neutrality, "The rights of neutrality will only be respected when they are defended by an adequate power," and he pointed out how all sections of the country would benefit from the existence of a navy.[12] Elaborating on this theme, Hamilton advocated "dock-yards and arsenals; and for the defense of these, fortifications, and probably garrisons" until the infant navy was capable of protecting those facilities.[13] Madison argued that "as her Union will be the only source of her maritime strength, so this [the navy] will be a principal source of her security against danger from abroad," and could "never be turned by a perfidious government against our liberties."[14] Jay stressed the need for unity of effort in maritime development, with "navigation" and "fleets" functioning together to promote national greatness.[15] Opponents of these views, the anti-federalists, consisted of two groups: one envisioning the American future in westward expansion, eschewing overseas ventures and seeking internal development; the other determined to maintain existing boundaries and a more locally autonomous governmental structure.[16]

Which local interests were to be subordinated to other local interests or to a broader concept of the national interest formed the basis for much disagreement. Proponents of the Constitution believed the nation's future depended on maritime development. The joint imperatives of defense and economic vitality were compelling arguments to the Federalists, who considered a navy essential to their attainment. The destiny of the United States, in their view, was to be achieved on the land *and* on the sea, with the latter assigned the major role it had played in colonial safety and prosperity.[17]

When the new government began to function in 1789 prosperity had returned. An impressive recovery had been made from the postwar economic depression, and overseas trade was thriving. The Washington administration was anxious to secure a commercial treaty with England to open the West Indian ports to American shipping, allow products to be carried in American bottoms, and to reduce import duties on American goods.[18] The United States was eager to improve commercial relations with other nations, resolve problems with the Barbary Powers, and induce Spain to permit navigation on the Mississippi.

Meanwhile, Congress was organizing the new government and creating executive departments in order of priorities, with State, Treasury, and War taking precedence. The control of naval affairs, which had been managed by the old Treasury Board under the Confederation, was placed with the Department of War—an "empty gift," as one writer put it, because there was no navy.[19] During Washington's first administration the War Department, under General Henry Knox, confined its naval activities to securing estimates on the cost of ships. Naval matters, when they were discussed at all by Congress, came up in the debates on revenue bills and the promotion of trade. Thus a proposal for a tax on salt to subsidize cod fishing as "a nursery for seamen" who would man a navy in time of war was supported on sectional lines. A militia plan submitted by Secretary Knox included provision for a naval force. In 1792 Congress did pass a militia bill that exempted mariners from service in the militia, apparently on the theory that a sailor's work in peacetime or in war was so similar that no standby organization of seamen was required.[20]

The absence of a navy seemed not to trouble the Congress unduly until Algiers and Portugal concluded a truce in October 1793, thus freeing the Algerian corsairs to intensify their raids on shipping in the Mediterranean and to pursue their prey into the Atlantic. While minister to France in the 1780s, Jefferson had urged the construction of a navy to subdue the Algerians. Adams, then in London, had counseled negotiation and tribute on the grounds that Congress was unlikely to appropriate the funds to build sufficient warships. Even if it did, he argued, the experience of European nations had demonstrated that force was seldom effective.[21] President Washington first called Congressional attention to "that particular branch of our trade which belongs to the Mediterranean" in his second annual message of December 8, 1790, without making specific recommendations. Congress, more concerned at the time with the Indian problem on the frontiers, debated only whether to appropriate funds to negotiate a treaty with Algiers or to ransom captives. It did not even consider whether a naval force should be formed to compel respect for the American flag.[22]

The most vigorous support for the creation of a navy came from Secretary of State Jefferson. In a report to the Congress on December 30, 1790, forwarded without comment by the

President, Jefferson presented the options of "war, tribute and ransom." The first choice would require a navy, an option that had considerable Federalist support but was opposed by Secretary of the Treasury Hamilton, who contended that the government could not afford the expense at that time.[23] The Portuguese truce with Algiers provided Jefferson with another opportunity to reiterate his concern over affairs in the Mediterranean, and his second report was forwarded to Congress by Washington in December 1793. The House quickly passed a resolution endorsing the creation of "a naval force, adequate to the protection of the commerce of the United States against the Algerine corsairs." Following a committee recommendation, the House voted to approve the construction of four ships of 44 guns each and two of 20 guns.

Debate over the bill brought forth all of the earlier arguments, and again differences were primarily along sectional and party lines. While the Algerian threat was emphasized, the issue was complicated by the outbreak of war between Great Britain and France in February 1793. British Orders in Council sanctioned impressment and placed food on the list of contraband goods. Decrees from Paris added to the problems of neutral trade. Divided American sympathies toward the antagonists affected the debate over the navy bill. Bitter exchanges included assertions that the vessels would not be adequate for the assigned task, would provoke retaliation, or would benefit one group at the expense of others. To ameliorate Republican opposition to the bill, a provision was incorporated to cancel authorization for warships in the event of a treaty with Algiers.[24]

Finally approved on March 27, 1794, the act provided for six ships to be built or purchased, and increased the firepower of the two smaller craft from 20 to 36 guns. The bill specified ranks and ratings, amounts of pay, and types of provisions. The administration decided to build rather than purchase the vessels, and the Department of War solicited and received plans for ships allegedly superior in speed, maneuverability, and overall performance to any of comparable gunpower afloat. Washington, catering to local interests and seeking the most practicable naval yards in terms of experience and availability of materials, assigned construction to six different seaports. He appointed commanding officers designate in June 1794, all of whom had served with distinction during the Revolution, to supervise the building of their respective vessels.[25] Delays were occasioned by difficulties in securing materials, for the supply of oak was slow in coming from American forests, and European imports were impeded by the war. Costs escalated, and none of the frigates was completed when the United States concluded a treaty with Algiers on September 5, 1795.

Washington, anxious to have a navy, urged Congress to continue the program envisaged by the Naval Act of 1794 notwithstanding its provision that the authorization for warships would be cancelled in the event of a treaty with Algiers. Washington stressed the unemployment that would result from cancellation and "the derangement in the whole system consequent upon an immediate suspension of all proceedings under it." This appeal to domestic repercussions rather than international advantages evidently overcame some resistance. Congress, after considerable debate—largely in the House—passed the Naval Act of 1796 authorizing the completion of three vessels instead of the six previously authorized.[26] The President's final exhortation for a maritime capability was delivered in an address of December 7, 1796, where he stated that "a naval force was indispensable" to protect commerce and secure respect for neutral rights, and he advocated "the gradual creation of a navy."[27]

Developments on the international scene had provided arguments for a navy even before the wars of the French Revolution posed a threat to American interests that dwarfed the Barbary depredations. The Nootka Sound controversy of 1790, when Spanish warships captured British vessels trading on the northwest coast, brought those two nations to the verge of hostilities and led Britain to reinstitute the impressment of seamen. Americans were not exempt from impressment, for proving one's nationality was difficult and there were few consular representatives abroad to protect American sailors. Americans also feared that war between the two remaining colonial powers in North America might involve the United States.[28] And Spain, in 1792, deployed a "fleet" of six galleys on the Mississippi to deter American expansion and deny use of the river to west-erners bringing their produce to New Orleans for reshipment.[29] Intensified Algerian raids and the outbreak of war between France and England in 1793 brought a renewal of impressment, and the belligerents' infringement on the American concept of neutral rights provoked vigorous protests from a government unable to protect its interests with more than words and trib-ute.[30]

The long-sought commercial treaty with England, signed by John Jay in 1794, was a disappointment. It sacrificed certain American principles regarding the rights of neutrals and failed to prohibit impressment. Moreover, the treaty disturbed the French, who saw it as a violation of the Treaty of Amity and Commerce of 1778 and of America's proclaimed neutrality.[31] Fortunately, the United States signed a treaty with Spain in 1795 that opened the Mississippi to navigation. Still, the overzealous French minister to the United States, Edmund Genet, outfitted privateers in American ports to prey on British merchantmen and established prize courts for captured vessels and cargoes.[34]

Caught between the two major adversaries, President John Adams dispatched three emissaries to Paris in an effort to resolve outstanding issues. When the mission failed, the Presi-dent, on May 16, 1797, sent to Congress a special plea for the creation of a navy. Elaborating on French violations of neutral rights and attacks on American commerce, he stressed the necessity for a navy to defend the United States, protect "com-merce on the Seas" and "at home," and urged "the establish-ment of a permanent system of naval defense" as being "req-uisit." Drawing on one of Hamilton's arguments in the Federalist Papers, Adams concluded with a wider appeal: "How-ever we may consider ourselves," he warned, "the maritime and commercial powers of the world will consider the United States of America as forming a weight in that balance of power in Europe which never can be forgotten or neglected."[34]

The President's request for a navy came shortly after the Congress, following bitter debate, had passed a bill in March 1797 appropriating funds for completion of three of the frigates that had been provided for in the Naval Act of 1794. The first of these vessels to be launched, the *United States,* slid off the ways in Philadelphia just one week before the President's message describing French depredations and appealing for a navy. After nearly two months of debate, on July 1, 1797, Congress approved a Naval Armament Act, which provided for the outfitting and manning of the three frigates under construction. Opposition, based on previous objections to naval capability, brought forth the added charge that the Federalists wanted a navy primarily to increase the power and prestige of the national government.[36]

On March 5, 1798, Adams broke the log-jam on naval legislation in Congress by releasing a letter from the American commissioners to Paris indicating the failure of the French government to recognize the envoys and begin negotiations. The distribution of the "X.Y.Z." papers the following month, which revealed the duplicity of the French government, further stimulated a groundswell of opinion for legislation to expand the navy and retaliate against France with force. Among the twenty laws passed between March and June was one creating a Navy Department, signed April 30, 1798, by the President. Another, approved April 27, authorized the building or acquisition of twelve small armed vessels. Successive acts in May and June provided for galleys and sloops, and in July Congress finally authorized the completion of the three frigates whose construction had been halted by the treaty with Algiers in 1795.[37]

Adams had succeeded in obtaining the desired legislation. But the government had no plans for effectively employing the navy, if and when the ships were ready for sea. Perhaps some thought that the demonstrated intentions of the government to possess warships would induce the French to modify their behavior, and visionaries may have contemplated fleet action with the enemy or reciprocal raids on French commerce. The latter was impracticable because the British blockade and destruction of French merchant ships had left little opportunity for American depredations.[38] Fleet action was ruled out by the French decision to rely on a *guerre de course* strategy and the unlikelihood that any American warships would be available for such an encounter. The question of American naval strategy was resolved temporarily by the act of May 28, 1798, which permitted the President to employ the Navy to capture armed French vessels operating along the coast with designs on American shipping. Congress also imposed an embargo on French trade, allowed American merchantmen to mount guns, and abrogated existing treaties with France. Then on July 9 Congress approved the capture of French armed vessels anywhere by warships or privateers, which the President was authorized to commission.[39]

The Navy Department, under the vigorous and imaginative leadership of Benjamin Stoddert, the first secretary, moved rapidly to acquire, outfit, and man warships. Congress adopted the rules and regulations for the Navy that had been prepared by John Adams in 1775 and had prevailed in the Continental Navy, although modifications were to be made during the naval war with France. The European conflict facilitated the recruitment of officers and enlisted personnel by reducing the number of merchantmen and placing many merchant seafarers ashore.

Perceiving that a navy required more than ships and men to operate them, the President and the Secretary of the Navy decided to establish strategically located government navy yards. Unable to obtain specific legislation, the President assumed that authority on the basis of the act providing for the construction of six ships of the line, each mounting 74 guns. The new national capital, Washington, D.C., was selected as the site for the first navy yard. Subsequently, additional yards were located at Norfolk, Virginia; Portsmouth, New Hampshire; Boston, Massachusetts; Philadelphia, Pennsylvania; and Brooklyn, New York. Instead of renting these facilities, as had been the earlier practice, Adams and Stoddert, through negotiation and purchase, acquired the land and built permanent installations. The legality of this action by the administration was questioned by some members of Congress, and the issue was raised during Jefferson's first term in office.[40]

The President and the Secretary of the Navy were of one mind on the indispensability of a navy in peace as well as in war, and they were committed to providing for its continuous organization, supply, and upkeep. The department's administrative structure consisted of half a dozen clerks and a messenger in the secretary's office, with a similar complement under an accountant whose position was specified by law and who was appointed by the President and confirmed by the Senate. Naval agencies at various ports were augmented to provide support for operating vessels, and land was purchased to procure oak for timbers. Most ship construction was performed by the government, although some was let out to private firms.[41] By the time the Quasi-War with France ended, the American Navy had commissioned forty-five warships, including three 44-gun ships, six 36s, one 32, four 28s, six 24s, six 20s, and four 18s. The remainder consisted of nine galleys and smaller craft, designed primarily for harbor defense.[42]

Although they agreed on the need for a navy, the President and the Secretary of the Navy did not always agree on the most effective means for its employment. Both gave priority to the protection of American commerce from French armed ships cruising in Atlantic coastal waters and the Caribbean. But Adams was unwilling to allow his fledgling navy to venture into European seas, either for escort service or to seek out the enemy. While Stoddert exercised administrative and operational control over the Navy, he sought, not always successfully, the President's approval for general, and in certain cases, specific dispositions.[43] On only one occasion did Adams permit any of his carefully hoarded warships to stray from North American waters. Trade with the Far East had developed considerably in the 1790s, and Adams decided in 1799 to dispatch two frigates to the East Indies to protect merchantmen waiting to sail for home. The *Congress* of 36 guns under Captain James Sever was dismasted in a gale soon after departure and had to return to port. The *Essex* of 32 guns under Captain Edward Preble successfully carried out its mission.[44]

Naval operations began with the sailing of the USS *Ganges* from Philadelphia on May 24, 1798. Acquired by purchase, this 24-gun vessel was the first of the post-Revolutionary Navy to be commissioned and get underway. Ordered to patrol the coast and protect American commerce, initially it was not authorized to capture French ships because such action had not received Congressal approval.[45] The *Ganges* was soon followed by the

Constellation under Captain Thomas Truxton and the 20 gun *Delaware* commanded by Captain Stephen Decatur. The latter captured the first French armed vessel, a privateer, off the coast of New Jersey. Brought into port and declared a prize, it was later incorporated into the Navy.

By the end of 1798 the American Navy was able to take the offensive against French vessels in the Western Hemisphere. With the onset of winter, which reduced the number of enemy ships operating off the Atlantic coast, the American vessels formed four squadrons to operate in the Caribbean. Deployed in strategic positions along the various passages between islands, these warships were so successful that insurance rates on merchantmen and cargoes fell drastically.[46] Meanwhile, Congress enacted legislation to increase the Navy, culminating in the Act of February 11, 1799, authorizing six ships of the line mounting 74 guns each. By now the costs of the Navy alarmed the Republican agrarian partisans, whose spokesmen, particularly Albert Gallatin, castigated a policy of taxing the farmer to promote the interests of maritime sectors.[47] This Republican opposition delayed but did not prevent the implementation of the Federalist program of naval pressure on the French government and friendship with Great Britain.

The President's dedication to a permanent navy was reaffirmed in a letter to his Secretary of State in September 1798. "Whether general war or a universal peace should take place in Europe," he wrote, "I think it is plain, that in either case we ought to be prepared at all points, especially with our floating citadels; for no peace they can make, however universal it may be, can be lasting."[48] Adams' prescience about the durability of peace in Europe is not surprising in view of his experience, and his emphasis on "floating citadels" as the essence of preparedness revealed his implicit faith in the Navy to defend the nation and its vital interests abroad.

While most of the American naval action during the Quasi-War with France involved the capture of French privateers, a memorable encounter took place between the United States frigate *Constellation,* commanded by Captain Truxton, and the French frigate *L'Insurgente*. Both were rated equally at 40 guns but the American frigate possessed greater firepower with larger cannon, as well as superior speed and maneuverability. Also, the French vessel was under orders not to fire on American ships, and uncertainty over the identity of each vessel confused the captains. Truxton began firing and continued with good effect, while his superior seamanship prevented the *L'Insurgente* from escaping or coming alongside to board. The French ship surrendered after sustaining considerable damage and casualties, while the *Constellation* suffered little damage and few casualties. The victory, widely acclaimed in the United States, brought prestige to the young Navy. Two men serving on the *Constellation* were destined to become naval heroes: the first lieutenant, John Rodgers, and midshipman David Porter. A year later Truxton, in the *Constellation,* encountered the French 50-gun frigate *Vengeance.* After a fierce battle in which both ships suffered considerable damage and the French captain tried unsuccessfully to capitulate, the combatants drifted apart in the darkness and neither prevailed.[49]

The performance and achievements of the American Navy during the Quasi-War were impressive. With only one warship at sea prior to the outbreak of hostilities, and no period for training and seasoning, these hastily commissioned vessels and inexperienced crews sailed and fought like veterans. Commerce was freed from French spoliation and trade was increased substantially. Some eighty-four prizes, mostly privateers, were taken and most were condemned by the American courts, bringing a good financial return. President Adams proudly reported on November 27, 1800, that the Navy had proven its value by "the great increase in revenue," and that "the measures of maritime defense . . . has [sic] raised us in the esteem of foreign nations."[50] The effect of the American naval effort on the French government is impossible to determine. But it is reasonable to assume a causal connection between American sea power, French overtures for peace, and the eventual compromise settlement of outstanding issues.[51]

Upon the signing of the Convention of 1800 with France, the Adams administration recommended that all naval vessels be sold except for thirteen frigates, six to remain in service and seven to be laid up and maintained in readiness at navy yards. Funds were requested to continue building six 74-gun ships of the line and to finish construction of navy yards. Secretary Stoddert, in his final report, stressed that with ships in commission and others available for rapid naval expansion, "confidence may be indulged that we may then avoid those wars in which we have no interest, and without submitting to be plundered."[52] These recommendations were incorporated in two Congressional acts of March 3, 1801, which, through administration initiative, resulted in the creation of a permanent peacetime Navy.[53] The task of implementing this legislation fell upon the new administration of Thomas Jefferson, which took office just as the troubles with the Barbary states were mounting.

NOTES

1. Merrill Jensen, *The New Nation: A History of the United States During the Confederation, 1781–1789* (New York, 1950), 83. The pitiful state of the Army is sympathetically presented in James Ripley Jacobs, *The Beginning of the U.S. Army 1783–1812* (Princeton, 1947), 13–39. The political controversy over a national army is detailed in Richard H. Kohn, *Eagle and Sword: The Beginnings of the Military Establishment in America* (New York, 1975). See also Weigley, *History of the United States Army*, 75–86; C. Joseph Barnardo and Eugene H. Bacon, *American Military Policy: Its Development Since 1775* (Harrisburg, PA, 1955), 47–70; and Harry M. Ward, *The Department of War, 1781–1795* (Pittsburg, 1962).

2. A detailed account of the sad state of the Navy is Stephen Tallichet Powers, "The Decline and Extinction of American Naval Power, 1781–1787," (Ph.D. dissertation, U. of Notre Dame, 1965), which stresses financial considerations. Attitudes of Americans of the time toward a military establishment are described in Arthur A. Ekirch, Jr., *The Civilian and the Military. A History of the American Antimilitarist Tradition* (New York, 1956), 3–24; and Louis Smith, *American Democracy and Military Power: A Study of Civil Control of the Military Power of the United States* (Chicago, 1951), 17–28.

3. James A. Field, Jr., *America and the Mediterranean World, 1776–1882* (Princeton, 1969), 3–38; Gardner W. Allen, *Our Navy and the Barbary Corsairs* (Reprint, Hamden, CT, 1965), 1–12; Ray W. Irwin, *The Diplomatic Relations of the United States with the Barbary Powers, 1776–1816* (Chapel Hill, NC, 1931), 1–36; Louis B. Wright and Julia H. MacLeod, *The First Americans in North Africa: William Eaton's Struggle for a Vigorous Policy Against the Barbary Pirates, 1799–1805* (Princeton, 1945), 1–15.

4. Washington to Hamilton, May 2, 1783, in Saxe Commins, ed., *Basic Writings of George Washington* (New York, 1948), 469. Washington also emphasized the defensive importance of control of the Great Lakes. Ibid., 469–470, 474–475.

5. Dumas Malone, *Jefferson and His Time: Jefferson the Virginian* (Boston, 1948), 316–317.

6. The quote is from Higginbotham, *The War of American Independence*, 444.

7. The most pessimistic view is John Fiske, *The Critical Period* (Boston, 1888). Less so is Jensen, *The New Nation*, previously cited.

8. Carlton Savage, ed., *Policy of the United States Toward Maritime Commerce in War* (2 vols, Washington, 1934), I, 157–160. The treaty concluded with Prussia in 1785 incorporated some of these provisions, as had the Treaty of Amity and Commerce with France in 1778. William M. Malloy, ed., *Treaties, Conventions, International Acts, Protocols and Agreements Between the United States of America and Other Powers, 1776–1809* (2 vols, Washington, 1910), II, 1477–1486.

9. Sprout and Sprout, *The Rise of American Naval Power*, 18–19. Jay, writing in 1785 on the news that Algiers had declared war on the United States, said "This war does not strike me as a great evil. The more we are ill-treated abroad the more we shall unite and consolidate at home." Quoted in Samuel Flagg Bemis, "John Jay," in Bemis, ed., *The American Secretaries of State and Their Diplomacy* (10 vols, New York, 1928), I, 269.

10. Burnett, *The Continental Congress*, 633. See his chapter XXXII, "Figs From Thistles, Congress and the Sea."

11. Max Farrand, ed., *The Records of the Federal Convention of 1787* (3 vols, New Haven, 1911), II, 135, 136, 158.

12. Edward Mead Earle, ed., *The Federalist: A Commentary on the Constitution of the United States* (New York, n.d.), 65, 67 [No. 11].

13. Ibid., 152 [No. 24].

14. Ibid., 266 [No. 41].

15. Ibid., 20–21 [No. 4].

16. Marshall Smelser, *The Congress Founds The Navy, 1787–1798* (Notre Dame, 1959), 19–20. The naval issue in the debates over ratification of the Constitution is covered in ibid., 5–21; Sprout and Sprout, *The Rise of American Naval Power*, 19–24; Smelser, "Whether to Provide and Maintain a Navy (1787–1788)," U.S. Naval Institute *Proceedings*, 83 (September 1957), 944–953; and John A. Rohr, "Constitutional Foundations of the United States Navy," *Naval War College Review*, XLV (Winter, 1992), 68–84, which stresses opposition and support for the constitutional basis for a navy.

17. Concern over external factors and national defense in the formation of a national government is stressed in Frederick W. Marks III, *Independence on Trial: Foreign Affairs and the Making of the Constitution* (Baton Rouge, 1973).

18. Jensen, *The New Nation*, 218.

19. Short, *The Development of National Administrative Organization in the United States*, 104. The quote is from Leonard D. White, *The Federalists: A Study in Administrative History* (New York, 1948), 157.

20. Smelser, *The Congress Founds The Navy*, 22–30.

21. The contention that these different solutions revealed Jefferson's enthusiasm for a navy and Adams' lack of support is challenged by James A. Carr, "John Adams and the Barbary Problem: The Myth and the Record," *The American Neptune*, XXVI (October 1966), 235–237. More information on the controversy may be found in John Joseph Kelly, Jr., "The Struggle for American Seaborne Independence as Viewed by John Adams," (Ph.D. dissertation, Univ. of Main, 1973), 249–263; Dumas Malone, *Jefferson and the Rights of Man* (Boston, 1952), 27–32. For Jefferson's attempt to get Congress to build ships see Julian Boyd, ed., *Writings of Thomas Jefferson*, X, 560–566.

22. James D. Richardson, ed., *A Compilation of the Messages and Papers of the Presidents* (20 vols, New York, 1923), I, 75, 76, 78. As Smelser puts it, "Reading the *Annals* of the first two Congresses one must conclude that the Algerine captives and the Mediterranean trade were among their smallest concerns." *The Congress Founds The Navy*, 43. Domestic priorities are emphasized in Gary E. Wilson, "The First American Hostages in Moslem Nations, 1784–1789," *The American Neptune*, XLI (July 1981), 221–223. Washington's reticence in making specific recommendations to Congress on military matters is noted by Howard White, *Executive Influence in Determining Military Policy in the United States* (2 vols, Urbana, IL, 1925), I, 85–86, 137–139.

23. Ibid., 136, 94.

24. Ibid., 139–142; Smelser, *The Congress Founds The Navy*, 48–63; Julia H. Macleod, "Jefferson and the Navy: A Defense," *Huntington Library Quarterly*, VIII (February 1945), 154–157; *Paullin's History of Naval Administration*, 89–93. The administration decision to adopt a neutral stance in the Franco-British war "was not arrived at without careful weighing of perplexing considerations." Charles S. Hyneman, "Neutrality During the European Wars of 1792–1815: America's Understanding of Her Obligations," *American Journal of International Law*, XXIV (April 1930), 281.

25. Those appointed were John Barry, Samuel Nicholson, Silas Talbot, Joshua Barney, Richard Dale, and Thomas Truxton. Barney declined because of an altercation over rank, and James Sever took his place. *Paullin's History of Naval Administration*, 95. For a comprehensive account, see Christopher McKee, *A Gentlemanly and Honorable Profession: The Creation of the U.S. Naval Officer Corps, 1794–1815* (Annapolis, 1991).

26. Richardson, *Messages and Papers of the Presidents*, I, 185; Smelser, *The Congress Founds The Navy*, 72–86. Details of construction are contained in Franklin D. Roosevelt, "Our First Frigates. Some Unpublished Facts About Their Construction," *Transactions, Society of Naval Architects and Marine Engineers*, XII (1914), 139–155. In commenting on the reduction from six to

three frigates (2 44s, 1 36), Roosevelt observed: ". . . it will be seen at this early date Congress failed to recognize the needs of the country, and by a half-and-half policy incurred in the end greater expense and less efficiency." Ibid., 145.

27. Richardson, *Messages and Papers of the Presidents,* I, 193. The role of Alexander Hamilton in encouraging the President to stress the need for a navy is developed in Smelser, *The Congress Founds The Navy,* 87–88.

28. James Fulton Zimmerman, *Impressment of American Seamen* (Reprint, Port Washington, NY, 1966), 30–35; Samuel Flagg Bemis, *Jay's Treaty: A Study in Commerce and Diplomacy* (New York, 1924), 53–55.

29. A full account is Abraham P. Nasatir, *Spanish War Vessels on the Mississippi, 1792–1796* (New Haven, 1968).

30. The British resort to impressment as a necessary method of manning the fleet is explained in G. J. Marcus, *The Age of Nelson: The Royal Navy, 1793–1815* (New York, 1971), 23. A less critical assessment is N. A. M. Rodger, *The Wooden World: An Anatomy of the Georgian Navy* (Annapolis, 1986). For early negotiations on the issue of impressment, see Zimmerman, *Impressment of American Seamen,* 43–45. John Adams' views are revealed in Kelly, "The Struggle for American Seaborne Independence as Viewed by John Adams," 263–264.

31. For negotiations on international law matters, see Bemis, *Jay's Treaty,* 232–251; and Daniel George Lang, *Foreign Policy in the Early Republic: The Law of Nations and the Balance of Power* (Baton Rouge, 1985). The French reaction is described in Albert Hall Bowman, *The Struggle for Neutrality: Franco-American Diplomacy During the Federalist Era* (Knoxville, TN, 1974); and De Conde, *Entangling Alliance,* 108–109, 376–378, 478–479.

32. Ibid., 201; Hyneman, "Neutrality During the European Wars of 1792–1815," 301–303. More detailed is Melvin H. Jackson, *Privateers in Charleston, 1793–1796: An Account of a French Palatinate in South Carolina* (Washington, 1969). Harry Ammon, *The Genet Mission* (New York, 1973), includes a discussion of the rights and duties regarding privateering under the Franco-American treaties.

33. The fullest treatment of the diplomacy of this episode is William Stinchcombe, *The XYZ Affair* (Westport, CT, 1980). Also see Alexander De Conde, *The Quasi-War: The Politics and Diplomacy of the Undeclared War with France, 1797–1801* (New York, 1966), 36–73. For French depredations on American merchant vessels, see Gardner W. Allen, *Our Naval War With France* (Boston, 1909, reprint, 1967), 28–40. The indispensable source is Dudley Knox, ed., *Naval Documents Related to the Quasi-War Between the United States and France: Naval Operations from February 1797 to December 1801* (7 vols, Washington, 1935–1938).

34. Richardson, *Messages and Papers of the Presidents,* I, 223–229.

35. Smelser, *Congress Founds The Navy,* 89–99. Again, opposition came from the Republicans. The act providing for the manning and employment of

the three frigates was signed by the President on July 1, 1797. *Naval Documents . . . Quasi-War*, I, 7–9.

36. Smelser, *Congress Founds The Navy*, 128–129. For the contention that Jefferson adopted the Republican anti-navy position during the years 1793–1801, see Joseph G. Henrich, "The Triumph of Ideology: The Jeffersonians and the Navy, 1779–1807," (Ph.D. dissertation, Duke University, 1971), 160–161. Henrich maintains that opposition to the navy was based on party, not sectional lines. Ibid., 91–98.

37. *Naval Documents . . . Quasi-War*, I, 59–60. The vote in the House on the bill to establish a Navy Department was 47 to 41, with most support from the north and most opposition from the south. *Paullin's History of Naval Administration*, 99–101; Sprout and Sprout, *The Rise of American Naval Power*, 38–39; De Conde, *The Quasi-War*, 90; Smelser, *The Congress Founds The Navy*, 133–138. Smelser contends that this flood of legislation authorized a navy for defense only. Ibid., 148.

38. Alfred Thayer Mahan, *The Influence of Sea Power Upon the French Revolution and Empire, 1793–1812* (2 vols, London, 1892), II, 259; Maclay, *American Privateers*, 219.

39. De Conde, *The Quasi-War*, 90–91, 101, 106; Allen, *Our Naval War With France*, 55–59. Adams commissioned 365 privateers. Ibid., 59. Instructions from Stoddert of July 10, 1798, "authorized, instructed and directed" United States armed vessels "to subdue seize and take any armed French Vessel, or Vessels sailing under Authority or Pretence of Authority from the French Republic, which shall be found within the jurisdictional Limits of the United States, or elsewhere on the high Seas . . ." *Naval Documents . . . Quasi-War*, I, 187. Concern that American sailors might be treated as pirates helped prompt the Congress to "declare" war. David LePere Savageau, "The United States Navy and its 'Half War' Prisoners, 1798–1801," *The American Neptune*, XXXI (July 1971), 160–161. John D. Pelzer, "Armed Merchantmen and Privateers: Another Perspective on America's Quasi-War with France," *The American Neptune*, 50 (Fall 1990), 270–280, deplores the emphasis on naval encounters to the neglect of privateers and merchantmen.

40. *Paullin's History of Naval Administration*, 113–116; White, *The Federalists*, 160. These navy yards did not have dry-docks or marine railways. Howard I. Chapelle, *The History of American Sailing Ships* (New York, 1935), 81.

41. White, *The Federalists*, 156–163; *Paullin's History of Naval Administration*, 105 ff. Overwhelming reasons for appointing a shipping merchant to the post of secretary of the navy are enumerated in Robert G. Albion, "The First Days of the Navy Department," *Military Affairs*, XII (Spring 1948), 3. For Stoddert's accomplishments see Robert F. Jones, "The Naval Thought and Policy of Benjamin Stoddert, First Secretary of the Navy, 1798–1801," *The American Neptune*, XXIV (January 1964), 61–69; John J. Carrigg, "Benjamin Stoddert, 18 June 1798–31 March 1801," in Paolo E. Coletta, ed., *American*

Secretaries of the Navy (2 vols, Annapolis, 1980), I, 59–75; John J. Carrigg, "Benjamin Stoddert and the Foundation of the American Navy," (Ph.D. dissertation, Georgetown University, 1953); and Robert L. Scheina, "Benjamin Stoddert, Politics, and the Navy," *American Mercury,* 35 (January 1976), 54–68. "If one had to characterize Stoddert's service it must be efficiency and a sincere loyalty to his Navy." Ibid., 64.

42. Allen, *Our Naval War With France,* 61–62. For a list of names, gunpower, and commanding officers, see ibid., Appendix IV, 301–303; and *Naval Documents . . . Quasi-War,* VII.

43. Kelly, "The Struggle for American Seaborne Independence as Viewed by John Adams," 300–305. As one writer puts it, "Adams exercised a direct command over the Navy . . . and was a very demanding Commander in Chief." William G. Anderson, "John Adams, the Navy, and the Quasi-War with France," *The American Neptune,* XXX (April 1970), 121.

44. Allen, *Our Naval War with France,* 141–161; Paullin, *American Voyages to the Orient, 1690–1865,,* 9–17.

45. Allen, *Our Naval War With France,* 63–64; Smelser, *The Congress Founds the Navy,* 180–181. For President Adams' employment of naval vessels in 1798, see Abraham D. Sofaer, *War, Foreign Affairs and Constitutional Power: The Origins* (Cambridge, MA, 1976), 149–159; and Gilbert Chinard, *Honest John Adams* (Boston, 1933), 287.

46. Allen, *Our Naval War with France,* 80–85.

47. The debates and the votes on the two naval bills are described in Sprout and Sprout, *The Rise of American Naval Power,* 47–49. For the establishment of the Marine Corps in 1798 and its role in the early Navy, see Allan R. Millett, *Semper Fidelis: The History of the Marine Corps* (New York, 1980), 23–45. A lively popular account is A. B. C. Whipple, *To the Shores of Tripoli: The Birth of the U. S. Navy and Marines* (New York, 1991).

48. Adams to Timothy Pickering, September 10, 1798, in Charles Francis Adams, ed., *The Works of John Adams* (10 vols, Boston, 1850–1856), VIII, 593.

49. A full account of the incident, including the reports of Truxton, Rodgers, and the French captain is in Allen, *Our Naval War with France,* 93–103. Also see Eugene S. Ferguson, *Truxton of the Constellation: The Life of Commodore Thomas Truxton, U. S. Navy, 1755–1778* (Baltimore, 1956), 160–169. For the engagement with the *Vengeance,* see ibid., 187–195.

50. Richardson, *Messages and Papers of the Presidents,* I, 302.

51. Allen, *Our Naval War with France,* 222; De Conde, *The Quasi-War,* 130. The "Convention of Peace, Commerce and Navigation" concluded on September 30, 1800, is in Malloy, *Treaties,* I, 496–505.

52. Stoddert assumed that the construction of six 74 gun ships of the line authorized by the act of February 25, 1799, would continue. He also recommended the replacement of smaller vessels and "the establishment of a Board, to consist of three or five experienced navy officers" to function under the

secretary, although such a board was not authorized until 1815. Stoddert to Harrison Gray Otis, Chairman of the Committee on Naval Affairs, January 15, 1801, *American State Papers: Naval Affairs,* I, 74–75. Earlier, Stoddert has suggested a force of "12 Ships of 74 guns as many Frigates, and twenty or thirty smaller Vessels . . . to inspire respect for our Neutrality in future European Wars . . ." He added, "On the American Continent we cannot have any enemy to excite serious aprehensions—in this particular we have nearly all the advantages of an Island & require the same kind of defense. It is from the European World that danger must come. A Navy alone can arrest it on its passage." Stoddert to Josiah Parker, Chairman of the Committee on Naval Affairs, January 11, 1800, *Naval Documents . . . Quasi-War,* V, 58–61.

53. The Federalists realized that significant reductions in ships and personnel were necessary in a peacetime navy. *Paullin's History of Naval Administration,* 118.

Chapter 4

The Barbary Wars

The naval policy of the Jefferson administration appears ambiguous and even contradictory. Based on a set of assumptions—strategic, financial, political, and philosophical—it reflected the Republican attitude revealed in previous debates over defense needs. Strategically, Jefferson believed in a navy for defense, not offense, "for such a naval force only as may protect our coasts and harbors from such depredations as we have experienced," as he wrote in 1799.[1] Further, a large navy designed for offensive operations would, he thought, be provocative, creating suspicion and hostility abroad. Commerce raiding was to be conducted by hastily commissioned privateers while small naval vessels defended the continent. Therefore, the composition of the navy was to be determined by its assigned mission and purpose.[2] Yet Jefferson came to realize that his initial prescription for defense might be inadequate. Writing in 1806, he stated, "The building some ships of the line instead of our most indifferent frigates is not to be lost sight of. That we should have a squadron properly composed to prevent the blockading our ports is indispensable. The Atlantic frontier," he continued, "from numbers, wealth, and exposure to potent enemies, have a proportionate right to be defended with the western frontier, for whom we keep up 3,000 men."[3] The type of ships against which the coast had to be defended should determine the composition of the navy, and the President had to consider coastal and international trade lanes as well as blockade or invasion points. That the primary mission of the Navy ought not be to influence or coerce the behavior of other nations may have been the strategic basis for Republican opposition to a large navy, as has been contended, although Jefferson was not averse to doing so on occasion, as in the Mediterranean to protect American commerce.[4]

Financially, Jefferson and his Secretary of the Treasury Albert Gallatin reflected the Republican fiscal policy of reducing federal expenditures and taxes, and of balancing the budget. Large budgets and indebtedness worked an economic hardship on the people and politically enhanced the power of the government, both anathema to the party of agrarianism and decentralization.[5] Philosophically, war and instruments of war were considered detrimental to those humane pursuits conducive to the better nature of humankind. Peace would best be served by reducing tensions among nations, not by a navy designed for intimidation.[6]

On assuming office Jefferson had no illusions about his expertise in naval matters. The Navy Department, he wrote, "is the department I understand the least, and therefore need a person whose complete competence will justify the most entire confidence and resignation."[7] The quest for a secretary was complicated by the presidential election of 1800, which ultimately placed the choice in the House of Representatives, and the issue was not decided until February 20, 1801. Meanwhile, Jefferson had persuaded a reluctant Benjamin Stoddert to remain in the office until a replacement was found, and it was he who began disposing of ships under the legislation of March 3, 1801. Eventually Jefferson appointed Robert Smith, an admiralty lawyer from Baltimore, whose acquaintance with the sea was more vicarious than real. Yet Smith had a keen mind, important contacts in Congress, and a commitment to the navy's welfare. His successive recommendations, often conflicting with his Treasury colleague Gallatin, reveal an understanding and appreciation of the role that naval power could play in the future of the country, both for territorial defense and the implementation of commercial opportunities and other national interests abroad.[8] During his tenure as Secretary, Smith was ably assisted by his chief clerk, Charles Goldsborough, who served in the department almost continuously from 1798 to 1842.

While the selection of a secretary of the Navy could be deferred, action on deteriorating relations with the Barbary states could not. Consisting of Morocco, Algiers, Tunis, and Tripoli, these countries occupied the Northern tier of Africa from Gibraltar to Egypt. By controlling the trade routes in the Mediterranean they derived their income from preying on merchant vessels or exacting tribute and "gifts" from other nations. Existing treaties with the United States had brought an uneasy measure of safety to American commerce. But American deliveries of money and naval stores to the Barbary states had been delayed because of the Quasi-War with France, and complaints from the corsair rulers had become threatening. Access to Mediterranean ports was vital to the American economy, and the Napoleonic wars had enabled neutral America to acquire a larger share of the world's carrying trade, a trade that contributed to prosperity and provided revenues for the debt-ridden government.[9]

Humiliating corsair behavior reached a new high in the case of the American frigate *George Washington* under Captain William Bainbridge. Ordered to bring money and supplies to Algiers as tribute and to investigate the state of affairs in the Mediterranean, the *George Washington* arrived at Algiers on September 17, 1800. After unloading and provisioning, Bainbridge was compelled by the Algerian government to sail for Constantinople carrying an Algerian emissary and a motley cargo, including animals as well as people. Protests and negotiations were fruitless and armed resistance was impracticable since the vessel was moored directly under the harbor batteries, so Bainbridge sailed to Constantinople. Following this bizarre odyssey the *George Washington* returned home, where Jefferson voiced no criticism of the apprehensive Bainbridge's conduct.[10]

In his dealings with the Barbary Powers, Jefferson possessed an instrument denied his predecessors, namely, a battle-tested peacetime Navy. He was therefore in a position to implement his earlier recommendation for employing force against the corsairs. The Act of March 3, 1801, under which the President was "*authorized,*" but not directed, "whenever the situation of public affairs shall in his opinion render it expedient, to cause to be sold . . . all or any of the ships and vessels belonging to the navy," excepting thirteen specified frigates, six of which were to be "kept in constant service" and the remainder "laid up in convenient ports."[11] Nonetheless, Jefferson immediately directed compliance, suspended the building of six 74-gun ships of the line previously authorized, and halted the construction of all navy yards except the one at Washington.[12] During his first year in office, he reduced the Navy from 21 frigates, 3 brigs, 3 ships, 2 schooners, and some galley-type gunboats, to 13 frigates and 1 schooner.

While the Navy was being reduced in size and composition, Jefferson faced the dilemma of deteriorating relations with the Barbary states. American consular officials had been reporting unsatisfactory negotiations and unreasonable demands. Affairs had reached the point where the Adams administration had intended to send a naval squadron to the Mediterranean when the war with France was terminated, and Jefferson lost no time in doing so.[13] The experienced Captain Thomas Truxton, selected to command the squadron, refused when denied authority "to act decisively against the Algerines." The purpose of an American naval presence in the Mediterranean, Truxton was told, was threefold: to train young officers, to employ the ships in accordance with the Act of 1801, and to serve as a deterrent. As the official letter put it, "It is conceived also that such a squadron Cruzing [sic] in view of the Barbary Powers will have a tendency to prevent them from seizing on our Commerce, whenever Passion or a Desire of Plunder might Incite them thereto."[14] After Truxton's refusal, command of the squadron was assigned to Captain Richard Dale, who had served with John Paul Jones during the Revolution.

Instructions to Dale, now addressed as Commodore in keeping with his assignment, were comprehensive and detailed. He was to command a squadron of four vessels, the frigates *President* (44), *Philadelphia* (36), and *Essex* (32), and the schooner *Enterprise* (12). Training, discipline, and showing the flag were emphasized. Most specific were portions of his orders concerning his conduct toward the Barbary nations. If, on arrival at Gibraltar, he should find a "tranquil" situation, he was to visit the Barbary ports, deliver tribute and mail, and promise future deliveries. But if he should find that the Barbary Powers had declared war against the United States, "you will then distribute your force in such manner as your judgment shall direct, so as best to protect our commerce & chastize their insolence—by sinking, burning or destroying their ships & vessels wherever you shall find them." Under no circumstances was he to "permit the public armed Vessel under your command to be detained or searched, nor any of the officers or men belonging to her to be taken from her, by the Ships or Vessels of any Foreign Nation, so long as you are in a Capacity to repel such Outrage on the honor of the american [sic] Flag."[15] Neither disrespect nor humiliation was to be tolerated.

Prior to the issuance of Dale's orders Jefferson held a cabinet meeting on May 15, 1801. Concerned about his constitutional prerogatives, he solicited advice on action he could direct if American vessels were attacked or war was declared against the United States. Unanimous in supporting Dale's mission, all of the cabinet members agreed that the President could authorize defense, and only Attorney General Levi Lincoln demurred on the destruction of enemy ships.[16]

This first of many American squadrons to be stationed abroad arrived at Gibraltar on July 1, 1801.[17] Finding two Tripolitan warships in port, Dale prudently assigned the *Philadelphia* to watch them, although he was unaware that the Pasha had declared war on the United States the preceding month. After detaching the *Essex* to escort merchantmen, he sailed to Algiers with the *President* and the *Enterprise*, and there he learned that war had been declared by Algiers. Proceeding to Tunis, where he was joined by the *Essex*, he took the three ships to Tripoli. There Dale had a written exchange with the Pasha, the American consul having been expelled. The Pasha wanted to negotiate peace terms. Since the Commodore had no authority to do so, nothing was resolved. After eighteen unproductive days the squadron got underway to Malta for fresh water.[18]

Enroute to Malta, the *Enterprise*, Lieutenant Andrew Sterrett commanding, sailing alone encountered a Tripolitan polacca. Sterrett, deceptively flying a British flag, learned that the polacca was hunting American merchantmen. Running up his true colors, he engaged the Tripolitan. Almost evenly matched in gunpower and numbers of personnel, the combatants poured shot and shell at each other for three hours at, as Sterrett put it in his report, "pistol range." Twice the polacca signaled surrender only to resume fighting, a ruse to lull the American close enough to board her. Sterrett's tactics were intended to prevent boarding, while remaining at close quarters for raking the enemy with gunfire. Skillful maneuvering and superior seamanship combined with effective gunnery to prevail. The Tripolitan, reduced to one sail and its guns thrown overboard, was allowed to depart because Sterrett's orders did not permit him to capture. The *Enterprise* suffered no casualties or significant damage, while the enemy had twenty dead and thirty wounded. Sterrett and his crew were duly rewarded by a grateful Congress.[19]

Little more was accomplished during Dale's cruise. Activities included an intermittent blockade of Tripoli, the escorting of American merchantmen, a missed opportunity to capture the crews of the two Tripolitan ships in Gibraltar [they had abandoned their ships and escaped], and a damaged keel repaired at Toulon. Prevented by his orders from taking the initiative, Dale was unable to bring matters to a satisfactory conclusion. Shortages of food and water caused sickness among his crew, enlistments were expiring, and the logistics of supporting a squadron abroad had not been solved. The Commodore sailed for home on March 9, 1802, leaving two frigates, the *Essex* and the recently arrived *Boston,* to patrol in the Mediterranean. Dissatisfaction in Washington led to Dale's resignation from the Navy, and he has been criticized for not taking more vigorous action against Tripoli. Accused of "dilatoriness," a more accurate assessment of Dale was made by James Fenimore Cooper, who labeled him "a man of singular simplicity and moderation."[20] The discretion allowed naval officers on distant stations because of the months involved in communicating with Washington was not sufficient to permit a moderate man to deviate from the explicit instructions governing his conduct.

Jefferson, hampered by restrictions on his use of the Navy in the Mediterranean, appealed to Congress. His first annual message, on December 8, 1801, emphasized trouble with Tripoli, "the least considerable of the Barbary States," and the inability to exploit naval superiority. "The Legislature," he concluded, "will doubtless consider whether, by authorizing measures of offense also, they will place our forces on an equal footing with that of the adversaries."[21] Six days later Representative Samuel Smith, brother of the Secretary of the Navy, offered a resolution to empower the President "by Law, further and more effectually to protect the commerce of the United States against the Barbary Powers." Following considerable debate, the "Act for the Protection of the commerce and seamen of the United States Against the Tripolitan Cruisers" became effective on February 6, 1802. The President now could initiate the use of force to protect commerce, and he could commission privateers and allow the taking of prizes. This legislation also extended the one year enlistment period to two, thus alleviating a problem that had plagued Dale.[22]

Armed with these new powers, Jefferson dispatched a replacement squadron to the Mediterranean. Again Truxton was offered command and again he declined, on this occasion because an officer with the rank of captain would not be placed in command of his flagship. This, Truxton believed, would amount to his accepting a reduction in rank. The assignment fell to Captain Richard V. Morris, commander of the *Adams* during the Quasi-War with France, whose squadron would consist of five frigates and the venerable *Enterprise*. Departing on different dates in the spring of 1802, these vessels joined the two frigates which Dale had left in the Mediterranean, making a total of eight men-of-war to conduct the mission.

The orders issued to the commander of this second Mediterranean squadron reflected the February 1802 legislation and the unstable situation in the Barbary periphery. Morris was "authorized and directed" by the President "to subdue, seize, and make prize of all" Tripolitan ships and goods. By Secretary of the Navy Smith, he was directed to blockade enemy ports, protect American merchantmen, exchange prisoners, and participate in peace negotiations. Morris was further enjoined "to contribute your utmost endeavors to effectuate without delay an honorable accommodation with Tripoli, Morocco, and any other of the Barbary Powers, with whom we may happen to be at war."[23]

The Emperor of Morocco, who had declared war on the United States, was the first of the Barbary rulers to be visited by the new squadron. He was both impressed by the formidable display and mollified by the promise of gifts and the granting of permission to send grain to Tripoli.[24] But Morris was not able to bring about the desired peace with Tripoli, the major adversary.

The Commodore, constantly beset by problems, never brought the full power of his command to bear on the enemy. His ships, not properly outfitted before leaving the states, often were laid up for repairs. Provisions were available only at Gibraltar, 1500 miles from Tripoli, for supply ships would not venture into the unsafe Mediterranean, and Malta was the nearest port for fresh water. The Navy Department simply had not developed a satisfactory system for logistical support of the squadron. Establishing credits for local purchases and sending out supply ships did not suffice, and only the later establishment of naval agents and depots abroad solved the problem.[25] The Commodore received frequent appeals from American consuls at Barbary capitals for the presence of men of war, which, together with the duties of escorting merchantmen and covering more than 3,000 miles of coastline, dispersed his ships. Moreover, exasperating delays in correspondence with Washington inhibited his actions. Effective blockade of Tripoli was virtually impossible, for small corsairs hugged the shores and eluded the larger American vessels. Weather, too, was a factor, especially during the winter season. Commodore Morris sailed from Malta for Tripoli with three frigates on January 30, 1803, only to be turned back by storms. His plan, if peace overtures had failed, was to launch a night attack with small boats to burn Tripolitan ships.

The Spring of 1803 brought improved weather and the completion of repairs, so the Commodore readied his squadron for action. The frigate *John Adams,* Captain John Rodgers commanding, captured a 20-gun Tripolitan ship, the *Meshuda,* and on May 20 Morris with the *New York, John Adams,* and *Enterprise* got underway for Tripoli. On arrival they saw a number of grain feluccas escorted by gunboats about to enter the port. The *New York,* giving chase, separated the convoy, but the gunboats reached the harbor and the safety of the shore batteries, while the coastal vessels took refuge in an adjacent port where the crews erected breastworks. The following day Lieutenant David Porter led 50 men in nine small boats in a foray to destroy the coastals. Supported by ships' batteries and amidst heavy hostile gunfire, his forces landed and set fire to the feluccas, only to see them saved when the Tripolitans extinguished the flames. The assault was carried out with commendable bravery by officers and men, who suffered about a dozen casualties.[26] When a subsequent attack on the gunboats by three frigates was thwarted by light and contrary winds, the Commodore opened negotiations with the Tripolitan government. Unable to agree on terms, the Commodore ordered resumption of the blockade of the port, with Captain John Rodgers as senior officer present in the *John Adams,* while Morris returned to Malta.

The monotony of blockade was broken on the evening of June 21 when the *Enterprise* sighted a large polacre and drove it into an inlet. Joined by the *John Adams,* the two ships fired repeatedly at the Tripolitan until it surrendered and then blew up.[27] Subsequently Morris raised the blockade and, relieved of his command, returned home. Both Secretary Smith and President Jefferson were displeased with the squadron's performance. Smith believed that Morris had "not done that which ought to have been done," and Jefferson authorized a court martial. But the Secretary settled for a Court of Inquiry, which found Morris "censurable for his inactive and dilatory conduct of the squadron under his command," and he was dismissed from the service. Perhaps the finding and dismissal were unfair, and a court martial might have enabled the Commodore to exonerate himself. At least he felt that he had performed to the best of his ability under almost impossible circumstances, circumstances that he was unable to overcome.[28]

With Morris's departure Captain Rodgers assumed temporary command of forces in the Mediterranean until relieved by Commodore Edward Preble. The new commodore, a veteran of the Revolutionary War, the merchant service, and the war with France, hoisted his broad pennant on the *Constitution* and arrived in Gibraltar with this third squadron on September 12, 1803. Under orders similar to those of his predecessor, he scoffed at moderation and was determined to be more vigorous in their implementation. His squadron was augmented by several schooners of 12 to 16 guns, authorized by the Act of February 28, 1803. These smaller craft permitted more effective pursuit of corsairs into shallow waters, and Preble was allowed to purchase two small vessels of "about 40 or 50 tons" for "reconnoitering" and "capturing some valuable prizes."[29] But Jefferson had decided, with the advice of his cabinet, to "buy a peace of Tripoli," and on board Preble's ship was Tobias Lear, the new Consul General at Algiers, with authority to negotiate a peace with Tripoli.[30]

On arriving at Gibraltar Preble learned of trouble with Morocco, so he persuaded Rodgers to defer his departure for home and join in a naval display at Tangiers. Other vessels were sent to blockade Tripoli, escort merchantmen, and capture Moroccan cruisers. The joint force appeared before Tangiers the same day that the Emperor arrived with a large army, but Preble and Lear were able to conclude a reaffirmation of the 1786 treaty. The Emperor's cordiality, effusive explanations, and anxious agreement were, the Commodore and others believed, due to the impressive presence of warships and Preble's own resolute behavior.[31]

While Preble negotiated in Tangiers two of his vessels blockaded Tripoli. The frigate *Philadelphia* (36), under the disgraced Captain William Bainbridge, and the schooner *Vixen*, Lieutenant John Smith commanding, arrived on station after escorting merchantmen and provisioning at Malta. The *Vixen*, the Commodore told both commanding officers, should be sent "well in shore to look into the bays and snug places along the coast."[32]

While on station Bainbridge heard of two Tripolitan cruisers at sea and, ignoring Preble's order that no fewer than two ships be on a blockade, dispatched the *Vixen* to search. The *Philadelphia,* blown off station by a storm, was attempting to regain position when, on October 31, 1803, a xebec was sighted making for port. Bainbridge, in hot pursuit, came almost within range but his volleys fell short. Approaching the fort's batteries and shallow water, he broke off the action and headed for the open sea. Unfortunately, he changed course too soon, for the *Philadelphia* struck the reef and settled at an angle, with water fore and aft and her bow raised some six feet higher in the air. Efforts to free the frigate seemed to worsen her predicament, and a heavy swell made her list to port. Observing gunboats approaching, Bainbridge threw overboard useless guns, anchors, rigging, and drinking water, all to no avail. The Tripolitan gunboats were positioned to prevent the *Philadelphia*'s remaining guns from bearing and to deny the use of ship's boats to move the frigate. Yet their attack was sporadic and halfhearted, with firing concentrated on the rigging in the expectation of capturing a sound hull. Four hours after the ship grounded Bainbridge held council with his officers. All agreed that it was impossible to refloat the vessel, that further resistance was useless, and that surrender was the only alternative. In an effort to scuttle the frigate the crew flooded the magazines, bored holes in the bottom, and broke the pumps. Guns were disabled and signal books were destroyed. The more than 300 crewmen taken captive were robbed, brought ashore, and imprisoned, an ordeal that was to last nineteen months. Within two days the Tripolitans, aided by a strong wind, had refloated the hulk and begun repairs.[33]

The loss of his ship compounded Captain Bainbridge's earlier humiliation while commanding the *George Washington,* and he spent much of his time in captivity disconsolately writing copious letters explaining the circumstances, defending his conduct, and suggesting methods of rectifying the situation. Some of his correspondence went via neutral intermediaries, and some, written in code or with lime juice, were smuggled out. A subsequent court of inquiry, held on board the *Constitution* at Syracuse, June 29, 1805, found that he had "acted with fortitude and conduct [sic] . . . and that no degree of censure should attach itself to him from that event." "In this opinion," the historian Allen concludes, "the government and the people concurred."[34] Furloughed to enter the merchant service, Bainbridge returned to the Navy in 1808 and served with distinction until his retirement.[35]

Commodore Preble, left with only one frigate and a miscellany of smaller craft, officially reacted with sympathy and understanding to the plight of Bainbridge and his crew. Privately, however, he allowed his personal feelings and irrascibility to denounce their surrender and expressed the wish that all hands had died in the action. His plans for a vigorous offensive disrupted, Preble instituted a blockade of Tripoli and sought to prevent the *Philadelphia* from being used by the enemy. Ruling out as impracticable an attempt to recapture the frigate, Preble decided that destruction by burning was most feasible, an action also urged by Bainbridge. The plan called for Lieutenant Stephen Decatur, then commanding the *Enterprise,* to take a volunteer crew aboard the *Intrepid,* a captured Tripolitan bomb ketch, and enter Tripoli harbor escorted by the *Siren,* a 16-gun brig. Then, his orders stated, he was to "board the *Philadelphia,* burn her and make good your retreat with the *Intrepid,* if possible, unless you can make her the means of destroying the enemy's vessels in the harbor, by converting her into a fire ship for that purpose, and retreating in your boats and those of the *Siren.*"[36]

The first two attempts were thwarted by bad weather, and Decatur feared that the element of surprise had been lost. Determined not to abort the venture, Decatur found a favorable breeze on February 16th and headed the *Intrepid,* disguised as Maltese, for the harbor. An Arabic speaking crew member obtained permission for the vessel to tie up alongside the *Philadelphia,* although its true identity was detected as the ships came together. Shouting "board," Decatur led his men onto the frigate and quickly subdued the guards. Designated squads placed combustibles in prescribed areas and, on the order "fire," applied torches. Hastily returning to the ketch, they barely escaped the roaring inferno and Tripolitan gunnery from shore batteries and cruisers afloat. With only one casualty, a crewman wounded in boarding the *Philadelphia*, the mission was accomplished, an exploit Admiral Horatio Nelson called "the most bold and daring act of the age." Commodore Preble, elated by the success, recommended a number of promotions, including that of Decatur to the rank of captain, a promotion quickly made. A grateful Congress awarded him a sword and the officers and crew of the *Interpid* two months extra pay.

The destruction of the *Philadelphia* infuriated the Pasha, who retaliated by raising his price for peace and for ransoming the prisoners. Preble, unwilling to accept the Pasha's demands, prepared to attack the port. Augmenting his squadron by small craft purchased, borrowed, or captured, he rendezvoused with the blockading ships on July 25, 1804. His entire force consisted of the *Constitution,* three brigs and three schooners each mounting 12 to 16 guns, six gunboats, and two bomb ketches. The defenses were formidable. On shore the forts and batteries were supported by an army of some 25,000 men. Afloat were a brig, two schooners, two galleys, and nineteen gunboats, all heavily armed and protected by the reefs.

The first of five assaults on the port was launched on August 3, 1804, in a classic example of what later was to be termed officially "restricted water operations."[38] The gunboats, divided into two divisions, were to enter the harbor with the bomb ketches, engage the enemy ships, and bombard the fortifications. Under covering support from the squadron's larger vessels, the tiny flotilla managed to survive the hostile fire and approach the targets as continuous volleys from cannon and small arms poured on the enemy. Three Tripolitan gunboats were boarded and captured in vicious hand-to-hand fighting, a tactic favored by the Barbary corsairs. Stephen Decatur found this type of combat "not child's play, 'tis kill or be killed." American casualties were three wounded and one dead, Lieutenant James Decatur, Stephen's brother. The squadron suffered minor damage while inflicting numerous casualties on shore and battering defenses and the town itself. Commodore Preble was satisfied with the results of the two hour battle despite some confusion over signals.[39]

Four days later, with repairs made and the three captured gunboats now part of the force, a second attack was launched. Although similar tactics were employed the outcome was not satisfactory. No enemy vessels were captured or sunk, and one American gunboat, her magazine hit by a hot shot, blew up with numerous casualties. As Preble broke off the action the frigate *John Adams* appeared with dispatches from home, one notifying him that Commodore Samuel Barron would be arriving with four frigates to assume command of the squadron. The President, Secretary Smith wrote, on hearing that the *Philadelphia* had been lost, "immediately determined to put in commission and send to the Mediterranean a force which would be able, beyond the possibility of a doubt, to coerce the enemy to a peace compatible with our honor and our interest." The Secretary apologized for replacing the Commodore, explaining that captains junior to Preble were not available.[40]

Preble, upset by being relieved at, as he wrote privately, "the moment of victory," decided to await Barron's arrival, for he believed that the combined forces could end the war with one coordinated attack. Then, on August 10, the Pasha offered peace on payment of $150,000 ransom for the *Philadelphia* prisoners. Preble countered by offering $100,000 for ransom and a $10,000 present, but the terms were rejected. Since Barron's squadron had not arrived, the Commodore, still hoping to conclude a peace, scheduled a night attack. Delayed by inclement weather and scurvy among the crew, the bomb ketches and gunboats bombarded the city on the night of August 24th with little apparent effect. The fourth attack, on August 28, employed tactics similar to those of the first two assaults with one major exception. The *Constitution,* under heavy fire from shore batteries, brought her own guns to bear on the Tripolitan vessels engaging the American flotilla. After sinking one boat, disabling two, and driving the others to shelter, the frigate moved closer to shore and fired hundreds of rounds of solid shot, grape, and canister at the fortifications, the castle, and the town. The Americans lost a ship's boat, three men were killed and one was wounded. Sails and rigging suffered damage and the *Constitution* had cannon balls lodged in her two foot thick hull. Preble was satisfied with the destruction inflicted on the enemy and his own relatively minor losses.

Still hoping to complete the mission before his replacement's arrival, the Commodore prepared for another assault, to be his fifth and last. On September 3 the gunboats and bomb ketches again led the attack, the former concentrating on the enemy galleys, the latter on the fortifications. The *Constitution* with the brigs and schooners—the latter finally able to get within range—battered the land defenses and other buildings ashore with impressive results. The American vessels had their rigging and sails damaged but suffered no casualties.

Not content with conventional tactics, Preble resorted to a fireship, hoping that it would destroy some Tripolitan galleys or one of the forts. The *Intrepid* was converted into a huge bomb, its hull filled with tons of gunpowder and its deck covered with shells and solid shot. The *Intrepid* was to enter the harbor at night and, when in position, the crew would ignite combustibles and escape in accompanying ship's boats. This bold plan was put into effect in the late evening of September 4. But, as the *Intrepid* with her band of volunteers entered the harbor passage, she was sighted by the Tripolitans and brought under heavy fire. Suddenly a tremendous explosion illuminated the scene and showered the harbor with metal and debris. The *Intrepid* had blown up with all hands. What caused the explosion has never been determined. Conjecture varies from Tripolitan gunfire to deliberate destruction to prevent capture.[41] A sixth attack, scheduled for September 5, was cancelled, for ammunition was nearly exhausted and weather conditions made gunboat operations hazardous.

Thus ended Preble's efforts against Tripoli. Convinced that blockade, escort, and chasing enemy vessels at sea would not bring the Pasha to terms, Preble had waged as vigorous a campaign possible with the resources available. Had he possessed the force assigned to his successor the outcome probably would have been different. His major regret was not having freed the *Philadelphia*'s crew. Nonetheless, the exploits of his squadron against strongly fortified Tripoli became legend and were never to be duplicated.[42]

Commodore Samuel Barron's arrival and relief of Preble on September 10, 1804, brought a formidable concentration of American naval power in the Mediterranean. The new squadron eventually included five frigates, four brigs, two schooners, one sloop, two bomb ketches, and ten gunboats. Barron, unlike Preble, was indecisive, unsure of himself, prone to temporizing and inclined to defer to others for advice. Stricken ill soon after his arrival, he relinquished command of the squadron to Captain John Rodgers, the latter's second time in this temporary capacity. Hoisting his broad pennant in the *Constitution,* Rodgers found himself committed on many fronts: supporting a land operation against Tripoli while blockading the port, patrolling the Mediterranean, escorting American merchantmen, watching a troublesome Tunis, recruiting crew members in Lisbon, and cooperating with two American special emissaries, William Eaton and Tobias Lear.

An overland operation was conceived by William Eaton, formerly consul in Tunis, who had persuaded President Jefferson to support an expedition to place Hamet Karamanli, the older brother of the Pasha of Tripoli, on the Tripolitan throne. The new ruler, presumably, would be more amenable to a satisfactory peace. Eaton had returned to the Mediterranean as a special agent with Commodore Barron, who had been directed to support his venture. The lines of command were somewhat confused. Lear and Eaton seemed to have overlapping authority to negotiate, although in certain respects both were subordinate to the Commodore. The military scenario envisioned a combined attack on Tripoli, the naval squadron by sea and Eaton's forces by land. Meeting in Egypt, Hamet and Eaton signed an agreement providing for American assistance to "reestablish" Hamet as ruler, declaring peace between the two countries, and reimbursement of the United States, from tribute exacted by Tripoli from other nations, for the cost of the war.

Eaton's heterogeneous army, comprising some 400 men of various nationalities, including eight American marines and a midshipman, left camp near Alexandria on March 8, 1805. Its destination was Derne, a city in Tripoli 500 miles away. The desert trek was hampered by a series of near disasters: shortages of food and water, desertions, mutinous behavior, bitter jurisdictional disputes, and hordes of camp followers who disrupted the force. Contact with American warships which were to supply provisions, arms, and money to pay the troops was often lost. Eaton, in a remarkable display of skill, tact, and resourcefulness, managed to overcome these obstacles. Finally the army camped on April 25. Aware that his force might dissolve and that a Tripolitan army was approaching, Eaton attacked two days later aided by the brigs *Argus* and *Hornet* and the schooner *Nautilus,* which poured heavy fire on the town and fortifications. By late afternoon a brisk defense had been overcome and the town was captured. Within days the Tripolitan army arrived and launched two assaults that, after bitter fighting, were repelled with support from ship gunfire. Then, on June 11, the *Constitution* arrived with news that peace had been concluded and with orders to evacuate the town. Hamet, his entourage, the Americans, and some Greeks were embarked on the frigate, leaving behind the remnants of their army. Eaton, disappointed at not fulfilling his dream of capturing Tripoli and distraught over what amounted to a betrayal of Hamet and his supporters by not deposing the Pasha, returned to the United States, where newspapers credited him with winning the peace.[43]

No doubt Eaton's expedition was a factor in ending the war, for the Pasha demanded the evacuation of Derne as a *sine qua non.* The American side of the negotiations, however, was conducted by the Commodore and Tobias Lear. Barron, confined at Malta while ill, had agreed that an attack on the port coupled with a tight blockade was necessary to obtain satisfactory terms. The assault was scheduled for the Spring of 1805 when the weather would improve, and Barron rejected an overture from the Pasha for negotiations during the delay. But in April the Commodore suddenly changed his mind. He cancelled the attack, agreed to negotiations, and announced that he was resigning his command and appointing Rodgers his successor. Ill health was one of many reasons he gave for his decisions, reasons that included a shortage of bomb ketches and gunboats, expiring enlistments, loss of faith in Hamet's cause, and fear that the *Philadelphia* prisoners would be killed in retaliation.

This precipitate action was a blow to his associates, who had looked forward to punishing the Tripolitans. But the authority to fight or parley rested with Barron, and he could not be dissuaded from his course.

The American negotiators, Lear, Barron and Rodgers, appeared at Tripoli accompanied by three frigates. The Pasha, admitting that he could not win an engagement, accepted a counter offer of no tribute, a man-for-man exchange of prisoners, and a ransom of $60,000 for the remainder of the *Philadelphia* crew. The Treaty of Peace and Amity, drafted by Lear, was concluded on June 4, 1805, and the American flag was hoisted on a new flagstaff at the consulate. Senate approval was not obtained until April 12, 1806, a delay that involved not only partisan political opposition by the Federalists but debate over the role of force and the American Navy in protecting and promoting the national interest abroad.[44]

Eaton denounced the treaty, claiming that the planned combined land and sea offensive would have compelled the Pasha to settle with no ransom. In retrospect there is little doubt that the terms amounted to a failure to utilize fully the naval force available in the Mediterranean. The squadron, already powerful when the agreement was made, was scheduled to be reinforced within two months by thirteen other vessels. Granting the impracticability of Eaton's proposed march from Derne to Tripoli commanding rebellious troops and opposed by the enemy army, the firepower and personnel of the squadron were more than capable of capturing the port. As for the fate of the *Philadelphia* prisoners, it seems unlikely that the Pasha would have killed them, for such an act would have brought fearful retribution and made a negotiated treaty impossible. If the Pasha had done so, one historian writes, "one may still be permitted to wonder whether Bainbridge and his fellows could have died in a nobler cause." Paying the ransom set a poor example, for it revealed that the United States was still susceptible to the kind of blackmail practiced by the Barbary nations.[45]

Peace with Tripoli brought little respite for Commodore Rodgers. The Bey of Tunis, angered by the capture of one of his vessels with two prizes while trying to run the American blockade of Tripoli and other alleged treaty violations, threatened war. First, however, the squadron sailed to Syracuse and Malta for provisioning and the usual repairs. While in port Rodgers dealt with other nations over ships taken during the blockade, talked with the British about deserters, supervised the *Philadelphia* court of inquiry, and paid off debts incurred by Eaton. On July 23 he sailed from Malta with Tobias Lear and seventeen warships, the largest American naval concentration to that time, and dropped anchor in Tunis harbor on August 1. Initially refusing to negotiate, the Bey changed his mind when Rodgers warned that more warships were coming and threatened a blockade unless the Bey signed an agreement to abide by the existing treaty. Negotiations resolved some outstanding issues and those remaining were left for discussion by an ambassador to be sent to Washington. Final items in dispute were settled by the United States paying $10,000 and returning three vessels that had been captured. This outcome can be attributed to the fact that Tunis was at war with Algiers, that the Tunisian ambassador had been impressed with his view of American resources while in Washington, and that the formidable presence of the American squadron commanded by the resolute Rodgers convinced the Bey that he could not get a better bargain.[46]

Peace with Tunis, President Jefferson declared in his sixth annual message of December 2, 1806, should be maintained "on equal terms or not at all," and added, "I propose to send in due time a reenforcement into the Mediterranean unless previous information shall shew [sic] it to be unnecessary."[47] Earlier, in his fourth annual message of November 8, 1804, he warned Tunis that to "those who expect us to calculate whether a compliance with unjust demands will not cost us less than a war we must leave as a question of calculation for them also whether to retire from unjust demands will not cost them less than a war."[48] Jefferson, too, calculated the factors involved in waging a campaign over "unjust demands." Restraining factors included expense, Congressional opinion, party doctrine, domestic reaction, the prospect of casualties, and the controversy with Great Britain over neutral rights during the Napoleonic wars. Against these restraints were the tangible and intangible ingredients of national interest. At stake were trade opportunities, honor, prestige, and respect accorded a sovereign nation. Concessions were repugnant, especially when believed unwarranted.

The President did possess the means to pursue a more vigorous military effort against Tripoli and Tunis had he wished to do so. That, as two historians concluded, "Jefferson did the best he could with the pitiful navy that Congress allowed him" is simply not so.[49] Preble and Rodgers each believed his forces were capable of compelling the Pasha of Tripoli to accept terms without payment of any kind, and Rodgers felt the same way about Tunis. As for Congressional support, when the administration requested authorization for "four small vessels of War, not exceeding 16 guns each" and some gunboats for closer inshore operations against the Barbary Powers, the legislation was immediately forthcoming.[50]

Jefferson employed force, with and without hostilities, to the extent he felt necessary to achieve an acceptable settlement of outstanding issues. Terms were negotiated, not imposed, naval strategy and diplomacy were coordinated, and the outcome was determined by the President. The Barbary problem was one of many that confronted Jefferson during his tenure as chief executive. His solution was consistent with his perceptions of the office, the nation, and the international scene.

Yet this compromise peace in the Mediterranean, concluded after years of half-hearted coercive measures, revealed glaring shortcomings in the government's naval policy. The gradual escalation and vacillation in applying force reflected the economy-oriented, anti-naval bias of the administration and its inability to understand fully the role of sea power. Initially, efforts were hampered by the drastic curtailment of ships and personnel and real or imagined Constitutional prohibitions. When Congress authorized action and the necessary resources they were not employed to maximum effectiveness. Facilities for building, repairing, and outfitting vessels were wholly inadequate. The navy yards, begun by the Adams administration, were stripped of personnel and equipment while effort was concentrated on the yard located at Washington. Appropriation for the continued development of the yards, provided by the Act of March 3, 1801, was not utilized. Vessels laid up in ordinary deteriorated from poor upkeep and required extensive overhaul when called up for service. The Navy Department, inadequately staffed, was overwhelmed by the multifarious dimensions of the Navy—the technicalities of ship construction, operations, logistics, recruiting, and budget. Secretary Smith, after nearly four years in office, admitted he had "not yet been able to acquire a taste for the details of the Navy Department," and Secretary of the Treasury Gallatin thought it might be impossible for naval affairs to be "conducted in reasonable terms."[51] The Jeffersonians, unprepared for contingencies, demonstrated an inability to provide for, administer, and employ the Navy to meet the crises when they arose in the Mediterranean.

The mounting cost of the Barbary campaigns led to the Act of March 26, 1804, which created what it termed "The Mediterranean Fund." Duties were added to all imports to "defray expenses . . . for carrying on warlike operations against the regency of Tripoli, or any other of the Barbary powers, which may commit hostilities against the United States."[52] Allocating revenue for a specific purpose appeared to alleviate the drain on the general budget, although these additional duties were anathema to the low tariff proponents. These supplementary funds accelerated the expansion of the Navy and its material support, but it did little to improve the quality of personnel to man the ships.

Recruiting qualified personnel was a constant problem, for life on board a man-of-war was not pleasant. The administration had reduced pay as an economy measure, and merchant seamen, unemployed because the European wars disrupted trade, preferred serving on privateers. The pay was better and signing on for a voyage had advantages over a term of enlistment. Maintaining discipline, always difficult with the heterogeneous crews and the primitive living conditions, became almost impossible on foreign station with months at sea and few decent liberty ports. Common infractions of the rules included desertion, mutinous behavior, assault, theft, drunkenness, homosexuality, insubordination, and improper performance of duty. Punishment was swift and harsh—a reprimand, confinement in irons and/or the ship's brig, or a stipulated number of lashes from the master at arms. The rigid command structure permitted a double standard in punishing officers and enlisted men for breaches of conduct, a situation not conducive to good morale. Popularly known as "Rocks and Shoals," the regulations for the governance of the Navy issued by President Adams in 1798 were superseded by regulations approved by Congress on April 23, 1800. Two years later President Jefferson issued a new set of rules that prevailed during his administration. No doubt many sailors agreed with Dr. Samuel Johnson, that "being in a ship is being in a jail, with the chance of being drowned." The man of war, as a floating gun platform, added military rigor and danger to an already miserable lifestyle that discouraged a career at sea for all but the dedicated.[53]

The absence of major altercations with the Barbary Powers and the decline in their infringements on American neutral rights led to a gradual reduction of American naval forces in the Mediterranean. Algiers proved to be the most troublesome corsair nation during the years 1807–1815, with the Dey complaining over payments and occasionally capturing American merchantmen. Cost was always a factor, and on May 15, 1807, Secretary Smith wrote angrily that "Hitherto the vessels which we have had in the Mediterranean have been maintained at an expense so enormous as to induce strong suspicion of an utter disregard to economy in the expenditure of publick money," and he ordered specific changes in procuring supplies, including the establishment of one central place of deposit.[54] Altercation and war with England further delayed a deployment along the Barbary coast, although when the war ended the American Navy was larger and more experienced.

Within days after Senate approval of the peace treaty with England, President Madison, on February 23, 1815, recommended war against Algiers. Congress responded with a declaration on March 2, 1815, and two squadrons were formed. The first to sail, under Commodore Stephen Decatur, left New York on May 20, 1815, composed of three frigates, two sloops, and two brigs. The flagship carried the new consul general for the Barbary states, William Shaler, who was named joint commissioner with Decatur and Commodore William Bainbridge, to negotiate for peace. At Gibraltar Decatur learned of an Algerian squadron cruising in the Mediterranean, and he began a search. First encountering an Algerian frigate of 46 guns, he immediately attacked. Skillfully maneuvering four of his vessels, he directed heavy broadsides at the enemy, which finally surrendered. American casualties were light and 406 prisoners were taken. Next an Algerian brig was sighted and chased into shallow water, to be followed by the American schooners and brigs where she ran ashore and was captured.

Encouraged by these initial successes, Decatur then sailed for Algiers with two options in mind. He hoped that the loss of the two vessels and the presence of the American squadron would induce the Dey to accept satisfactory terms. But if the Dey proved recalcitrant, Decatur intended to attack the shore defenses and the ships in the harbor. On arrival at the port the American commissioners insisted that negotiations be held on board the flagship, that the treaty not provide for payment of tribute, and that certain other demands be met. Within hours the Dey accepted the terms, prisoners were released, and American property was returned. The squadron then sailed to Tunis and Tripoli, where Decatur demanded and received compensation for American vessels that had been seized and turned over to the British. The Commodore then departed for home, and on the way rendezvoused with Bainbridge's squadron which had reached Gibraltar.

Bainbridge's flagship, the *Independence,* was a ship of the line mounting 74 guns, and with him were two frigates, one sloop, and two brigs. After showing the flag in various ports he joined the remainder of Decatur's squadron and departed for home, leaving a few ships to look after American interests in the Mediterranean under Captain John Shaw. Shaw and Consul General Shaler sailed to Algiers with the treaty that had been approved by the Senate and ratified by the President, only to discover that the Dey now refused to accept it, accusing the United States of bad faith. Shaw immediately prepared for a night attack, which he cancelled on learning that the Algerians knew of the planned assault. But the Dey, impressed by the

American resolve, changed his position. Still contending that the treaty was void, he offered to allow the Commodore to ask his government for instructions and permit Shaler to return to his consulate. The *John Adams* departed for America with a letter from the Dey to the President, and the squadron cruised about the Mediterranean visiting Barbary ports.

Meanwhile, in August 1816, a combined British and Dutch fleet bombarded Algiers and decimated the Algerian navy. In September the American squadron returned to Algiers, then sailed to Gibraltar where a brig had arrived with a letter from the President. Dated August 21, 1816, it appointed Shaler and the new commodore, Isaac Chauncey, as commissioners. Returning to Algiers in December, they presented the Dey with a virtual ultimatum. After trying to avoid receiving the ultimatum, the Dey accepted it with a note from Shaler saying he had done so under compulsion.

The treaty signed on December 23, 1816, ended the last major dispute with the Barbary Powers, although a naval presence was maintained in the Mediterranean until France annexed Algeria in 1830. Payment of tribute to any nation had ceased, although occasional "presents" were given to the rulers.[55]

The Barbary wars marked the coming of age of the American Navy. Trouble with Algiers had provoked the first peacetime naval program, the Quasi-War with France had put the new Navy to sea in combat, and action in the Mediterranean further demonstrated how armed force could and did protect American interests. This first American military venture abroad seasoned the Navy, enhanced its reputation, improved morale, revealed that it could operate effectively on distant stations, established logistic techniques, and provided experience in offshore and inshore operations, land assaults, and command tactics with two or more vessels. Fighting the corsairs produced legends and more heroes, and, again, revealed that the United States could and would defend its rights. The example impressed those European nations that had bribed the Barbary rulers for so long, and it enhanced the prestige of the young country. The successful outcome gave Americans a sense of pride and proved that the Navy was the essential first line of defense for the protection of citizens and property at home and abroad.

NOTES

1. Jefferson to Elbridge Gerry, P. L. Ford, ed., *The Writings of Thomas Jefferson* (10 vols, New York, 1892–1899), VII, 328. For the contention that Jefferson adopted the Republican anti-navy position during the years 1793–1801, see Henrich, "The Triumph of Ideology," 160–161.

2. Donald R. Hickey, "Federalist Defense Policy in the Age of Jefferson, 1801–1812," *Military Affairs*, XLV (April 1981), 63–65; Chapelle, *The History of the American Sailing Navy*, 241; *Paullin's History of Naval Administration*, 119.

3. Jefferson to Jacob Crowninshield, May 13, 1806, *Writings*, Ford ed., VIII, 453. "The regular Army of the United States owed its existence to the American frontier." Paul Prucha, *The Sword of the Republic: The United States Army on the Frontier, 1783–1846* (New York, 1969), 1.

4. Craig Symonds maintains that the Republican "antinavalists" merely opposed an "aggressive" naval policy, i.e., one of intimidation, threat, or deterrence. Craig Symonds, "The Antinavalists: The Opponents of Naval Expansion in the Early National Period," *The American Neptune*, 39 (February 1979), 24–25; and his *Navalists and Anti-Navalists: The Naval Policy Debate in the United States, 1785–1827* (Newark, DE, 1978), 86–89.

5. David Rich Dewey, *Financial History of the United States*, (10th ed., New York, 1928), 111, 124. "In a very real sense, Jefferson was the first 'economy' president." Lewis H. Kimmel, *Federal Budget and Fiscal Policy, 1789–1958* (Washington, 1959), 14.

6. See Reginald C. Stuart, *The Half-Way Pacifist: Thomas Jefferson's View of War* (Buffalo, 1978).

7. Jefferson to Samuel Smith, April 17, 1801, quoted in Henry Adams, *History of the United States of America During the Administration of Thomas Jefferson* (4 vols, New York, 1901), I, 242.

8. For Jefferson's long and difficult search for a Secretary of the Navy see Henrich, "The Triumph of Ideology," 178–199. Smith held the post, officially and unofficially, until March 1809. A succinct account of his life and achievements is Mary Wilhelmina Williams, "Robert Smith," Dumas Malone and Allen Johnson, eds., *Dictionary of American Biography* (22 vols, New York, 1946), XVII, 337–338. On his role as secretary, see George E. Davies, "Robert Smith and the Navy," *Maryland Historical Magazine*, XIV (December 1919), 305–322; Frank L. Owsley, Jr., "Robert Smith, 27 July 1801–7 March 1809," in Paolo E. Coletta, ed., *American Secretaries of the Navy* (2 vols, Annapolis, 1980), I, 77–90; and *Paullin's History of Naval Administration*, 119–135. That "Smith dealt with routine and with details; Jefferson and Gallatin with policy

and finance," is not quite correct for Smith did, through his political connections, influence legislation on ship construction and deployment. The quote is from Leonard D. White, *The Jeffersonians: A Study in Administrative History, 1801–1809* (New York, 1951), 271.

9. C. J. Marcus, *The Age of Nelson: The Royal Navy, 1793–1815* (New York, 1971), 121; Thomas G. Cochran, "The Business Revolution," *American Historical Review,* 79 (December 1974), 1455–1456; Dewey, *Financial History of the United States,* 110, 123. Wheat and dried fish were the major exports to Mediterranean countries. Thomas A. Bryson, *American Diplomatic Relations with the Middle East, 1784–1975: A Survey* (Metuchen, NJ, 1977), 2. Jefferson's enthusiasm for agricultural exports is emphasized in Joyce Appleby, "Commercial Farming and the 'Agrarian Myth' in the Early Republic," *Journal of American History,* 68 (March 1982), 833–849. For the view that Jefferson was concerned about overseas commerce solely to dispose of surplus agricultural products, see Alfred Thayer Mahan, *Sea Power in its Relations to the War of 1812* (2 vols, Boston, 1905), I, 187–188.

10. For Bainbridge's explanation, see Bainbridge to Stoddert, October 10, 1800, in Dudley W. Knox, ed., *Naval Documents Related to the United States War With the Barbary Powers: Naval Operations Including Diplomatic Background From 1785 Through 1807* (7 vols, Washington, 1939–1945), I, 378–379. Secretary of State James Madison wrote, "The sending to Constantinople the national ship of war the *George Washington,* by force, under the Algerine flag, and for such a purpose, has deeply affected the sensibility, not only of the President, but of the people of the United States." Madison to William Eaton and Richard O'Brien, May 20, 1801, ibid., 462. The incident is narrated in Gardner W. Allen, *Our Navy and the Barbary Corsairs* (Reprint, Hamden, CT, 1965), 75–87; Ray W. Irwin, *The Diplomatic Relations of the United States With the Barbary Powers, 1776–1816* (Reprint, New York, 1970), 94–95; Glenn Tucker, *Dawn Like Thunder: The Barbary Wars and the Birth of the U.S. Navy* (Indianapolis, 1963), 18–26; Louis B. Wright and Julia H. MacLeod, *The First Americans in North Africa: William Eaton's Struggle for a Vigorous Policy Against the Barbary Pirates, 1799–1805* (Princeton, 1945), 71–72; Leonard Guttridge and Jay D. Smith, *The Commodores: The U.S. Navy in the Age of Sail* (New York, 1969), 57–60. For local conditions, see William Spencer, *Algiers in the Age of the Corsairs* (Norman, OK, 1980); and John B. Wolf, *The Barbary Coast: Algiers Under the Turks, 1500 to 1830* (New York, 1979).

11. "An Act Providing for a Naval Peace Establishment, And for Other Purposes," March 3, 1801, in *Naval Documents . . . Quasi-War,* VII, 134–135. Italics added. The act also specified the daily rations for crews and the number of officers to be retained.

12. *Paullin's History of Naval Administration,* 125–132; Henrich, "Triumph of Ideology," 217; Jack Bauer, "Naval Shipbuilding Programs 1794–1860," *Military Affairs,* 29 (Spring 1965), 31–32. According to Bauer, "The Jeffersonian period is the nadir of the navy's construction program." Ibid., 32.

Another writer contends that "A good and respectable Navy could withstand much, but not Jeffersonian economy." Scheina, "Benjamin Stoddert, Politics, and the Navy," 64.

13. Secretary of State Thomas Pickering to American consul at Tunis William Eaton, January 11, 1800, quoted in Abraham D. Sofaer, *War, Foreign Affairs and Constitutional Power: The Origins*, 148; and Irwin, *The Diplomatic Relations of the United States with the Barbary Powers, 1776–1816*, 103–104. For an account of the altercations with the Barbary Powers that led to the dispatch of a squadron to the Mediterranean in 1801, see ibid., 92–102; and Wright and Macleod, *The First Americans in North Africa*, 61–88.

14. The quote is from Samuel Smith to Captain Thomas Truxton, April 10, 1801, in *Naval Documents . . . Barbary Powers*, I, 428–429. Samuel Smith performed the duties of Secretary of the Navy before the appointment of his brother Robert, while Secretary of the Army was *pro forma* acting Secretary of the Navy. White, *The Jeffersonians*, 270; and *Paullin's History of Naval Administration*, 121.

15. Dale's orders are contained in two letters of the same date, Smith to Dale, May 20, 1801, *Naval Documents . . . Barbary Powers*, I, 463–469. The honorary title "Commodore" was given to an officer in command of two or more ships. The rank was not established formally until 1862.

16. *Writings of Jefferson*, Ford ed., VI, 344–345; Irving Brant, *James Madison, Secretary of State, 1800–1809* (Indianapolis, 1953), 60. See the chapter "Jefferson and the 'Revolution of 1800'," Sofaer, *War, Foreign Affairs and Constitutional Power*, 207–227; and Charles A. Lofgren, "War-Making Under the Constitution: The Original Understanding," *The Yale Law Journal* 81 (March 1972), 672–702.

17. Robert Greenhalgh Albion, "Distant Stations," *U.S. Naval Institute Proceedings*, LXXX (March 1951), 266. This article covers the stationing of American naval vessels overseas to the establishment of the Sixth Fleet in the Mediterranean.

18. Charles Oscar Paullin, *Diplomatic Negotiations of American Naval Officers, 1778–1883* (Reprint, Gloucester, MA, 1967), 60–62. "With the tour of duty of this squadron, the diplomatic negotiations of naval officers with the Barbary powers had their beginning." Ibid., 58. Also see Allen, *Our Navy and the Barbary Corsairs*, 94–95. A valuable supplement to Paullin is David F. Long, *Gold Braid and Foreign Relations: Diplomatic Activities of U.S. Naval Officers, 1798–1883* (Annapolis, 1988).

19. Ibid., 95–97, which contains Sterrett's report; Irwin, *Diplomatic Relations*, 109–110; Guttridge and Smith, *The Commodores*, 64–65; Tucker, *Dawn Like Thunder*, 142–144.

20. "Dilatoriness" quoted in Guttridge and Smith, *The Commodores*, 65. Cooper quote in James Fenimore Cooper, *History of the Navy of the United States of America* (2 vols, Philadelphia, 1839), I, 341.

21. Richardson, *Messages and Papers*, I, 314–315. Allen is critical of

Jefferson's narrow construction of his powers, *Our Navy and the Barbary Corsairs,* 97, as was Alexander Hamilton. Dumas Malone, *Jefferson the President: First Term, 1801–1805* (Boston, 1970), 98. Malone writes, "He [Jefferson] had initiated a limited action, but its limitations were not owing to theoretical pacifism, nor chiefly to constitutional scruples, but to severely practical considerations" such as cost, public opinion, and insufficient naval strength. Ibid., 99.

22. Sofaer, *War, Foreign Affairs and National Power,* 212–216; Symonds, *Navalists and Antinavalists,* 93–94; *Naval Documents . . . Barbary Powers,* II, 51–52.

23. Ibid., 60.

24. Ibid., 65; Irwin, *Diplomatic Relations,* 114–116.

25. Davies, "Robert Smith and the Navy," 311–313; Field, *America and the Mediterranean World,* 460–461.

26. Allen, *Our Navy and the Barbary Corsairs,* 125–128; Guttridge and Smith, *The Commodores,* 69; David F. Long, *Nothing Too Daring: A Biography of Commodore David Porter, 1783–1843* (Annapolis, 1970), 21.

27. Captain Rodgers' report of the incident is printed in Charles Oscar Paullin, *Commodore John Rodgers: Captain, Commodore, and Senior Officer of the American Navy, 1773–1838* (Annapolis, 1909, 1967), 108–110; and Allen, *Our Navy and the Barbary Corsairs,* 129–131.

28. Ibid., 133–136; Christopher McKee, *Edward Preble: A Naval Biography, 1761–1807* (Annapolis, 1972), 105–122; Guttridge and Smith, *The Commodores,* 70; Paullin, *Commodore John Rodgers,* 111. The proceedings of the court of inquiry are in *Naval Documents . . . Barbary Powers,* II, 526–531. Morris published *A Defense of the Conduct of Commodore Morris During His Command in the Mediterranean* (New York, 1804), that contains copies of correspondence and other data.

29. Preble to Smith, July 16, 1803, quoted in McKee, *Edward Preble,* 130–131. The Act of February 28, 1803, authorized the building or purchase of "four vessels of war, to carry not exceeding sixteen guns each . . . for the protection of the seamen and commerce of the United States in the Mediterranean and adjacent seas, and for other purposes, as the public service may require." *Naval Documents . . . Barbary Powers,* II, 366. For size, design, characteristics, and the construction of these vessels, see Chapelle, *History of the American Sailing Navy,* 182–189.

30. The words are Jefferson's, quoted in McKee, *Edward Preble,* 129.

31. Ibid., 143–172, is a detailed account. Also see Irwin, *Diplomatic Relations,* 131–133; Allen, *Our Navy and the Barbary Corsairs,* 143–145; Paullin, *Commodore John Rodgers,* 112–114; and Tucker, *Dawn Like Thunder,* 201–208.

32. Quoted in Guttridge and Smith, *The Commodores,* 74.

33. Ibid., 74–80; Tucker, *Dawn Like Thunder,* 209, 218; Long, *Nothing Too Daring,* 22–24; Allen, *Our Navy and the Barbary Corsairs,* 145–153, which

contains Bainbridge's report to the Secretary of the Navy, November 1, 1803. Various first hand accounts of the incident may be found in *Naval Documents . . . Barbary Powers*, III.

34. Allen, *Our Navy and the Barbary Corsairs*, 105. The proceedings of the court of inquiry are printed in *Naval Documents . . . Barbary Powers*, III, 189–194. For a reassessment of Bainbridge, see Craig Symonds, "William S. Bainbridge: Bad Luck or Fatal Flaw," in James C. Bradford, ed., *Command Under Sail: Makers of the American Naval Tradition, 1775–1850* (Annapolis, 1985), 97–125.

35. Edward Breck, "William Bainbridge," *Dictionary of American Biography*, I, 504–507; David F. Long, *Ready to Hazard: A Biography of Commodore William Bainbridge, 1774–1833* (Ann Arbor, MI, 1981).

36. Quoted in Allen, *Our Navy and the Barbary Corsairs*, 166. The Commodore's reaction to the loss of the *Philadelphia* is detailed in McKee, *Edward Preble*, 179–183. The fore and aft schooner rig was occasionally changed to the square rig of a brig, and the reverse.

37. Ibid., 193–199; Allen, *Our Navy and the Barbary Corsairs*, 166–193; Guttridge and Smith, *The Commodores*, 85–90; Tucker, *Dawn Like Thunder*, 269–281. The possibility of towing the *Philadelphia* from the harbor safely is rejected by Tucker, 281, and Allen, 173–175.

38. Chief of Naval Operations to Commanders-in-Chief Atlantic, Pacific and European Fleets, Serial 0048P34, June 5, 1961, quoted in William R. Cracknell, Jr., "The Role of the U.S. Navy in Inshore Waters," *Naval War College Review*, 21 (November 1968), 65.

39. McKee, *Edward Preble*, 254–267; Allen, *Our Navy and the Barbary Corsairs*, 187–195; Tucker, *Dawn Like Thunder*, 293–305; Guttridge and Smith, *The Commodores*, 92–95.

40. Smith to Preble, May 22, 1804, *Naval Documents . . . Barbary Wars*, IV, 114–115.

41. McKee, *Edward Preble*, 303–306; Allen, *Our Navy and the Barbary Corsairs*, 208–209.

42. Preble's assaults on Tripoli are described in ibid., 187–211; McKee, *Edward Preble*, 254–306; Tucker, *Dawn Like Thunder*, 293–333; Paullin, *Diplomatic Negotiations*, 71–82; Guttridge and Smith, *The Commodores*, 92–100.

43. Wright and MacLeod, *The First Americans in North Africa*, 151–189; Allen, *Our Navy and the Barbary Corsairs*, 227–245; Tucker, *Dawn Like Thunder*, 350–413; Irwin, *Diplomatic Relations*, 143–148. Eaton's Proclamation to the Inhabitants of Tripoli and excerpts from his journal are printed in *Naval Documents . . . Barbary Powers*, V, 467–471.

44. Allen, *Our Navy and the Barbary Corsairs*, 248–266; Irwin, *Diplomatic Relations*, 149–160; Paullin, *Commodore John Rodgers*, 130–140; Tucker, *Dawn Like Thunder*, 415–428. The treaty is in Malloy, *Treaties, Conventions, etc.*, II, 1788–1793. Eaton's report of August 9, 1805, is printed in *Naval Documents . . . Barbary Powers*, VI, 213–218.

45. Irwin, *Diplomatic Relations*, 157–158; Charles E. Hill, "James Madison," in Bemis, ed., *American Secretaries of State*, III, 74–78; Brant, *James Madison: Secretary of State*, 308–310. The quote is from Irwin.

46. Irwin, *Diplomatic Relations*, 160–167; Allen, *Our Navy and the Barbary Corsairs*, 267–272; Paullin, *Commodore John Rodgers*, 141–159; Paullin, *Diplomatic Negotiations*, 90–106; Brant, *James Madison: Secretary of State*, 305–308, 310; Tucker, *Dawn Like Thunder*, 428–430; Guttridge and Smith, *The Commodores*, 105.

47. Richardson, *Messages and Papers*, I, 395.

48. Ibid., 359.

49. Wright and MacLeod, *The First Americans in North Africa*, vi.

50. Jefferson's second annual message, December 15, 1802. Richardson, *Messages and Papers*, I, 334; Secretary of the Navy Smith to William Eustis, January 18, 1803, *Naval Documents . . . Barbary Powers*, II, 346; Act of February 28, 1803, ibid., II, 366. Also, Congress responded favorably to Jefferson's request of February 10, 1807, for gunboats. Dudley and Crawford, eds., *The Naval War of 1812: A Documentary History, Volume I*, 12–15. Rodgers wrote the Secretary of the Navy that if the government decided to "chastise" the Bey of Tunis to "obtain an honorable peace" and "make him pay the expenses of the war," Rodgers could do so "with no more force than remains this winter in the Mediterranean." Rodgers to Smith, August 21, 1805, quoted in Allen, *Our Navy and the Barbary Corsairs*, 269–270.

51. Quoted in Dumas Malone, *Jefferson the President: Second Term, 1805–1809* (Boston, 1974), 36. For Navy Department administration, see *Paullin's History of Naval Administration*, 124–127; and Allen, *Our Navy and the Barbary Corsairs*, 215–217.

52. *Naval Documents . . . Barbary Powers*, III, 522–524.

53. Preble's severe discipline is detailed in McKee, *Edward Preble*, 221–227. The subject is explored in James E. Valle, *Rocks & Shoals: Order and Discipline in the Old Navy, 1799–1861* (Annapolis, 1980); and Frederick J. Bell, *Room to Swing a Cat, Or Tales of the Old Navy* (New York, 1938). Jefferson's set of rules has been reprinted, *Naval Regulations 1802 Issued by Command of the President of the United States* (Reprint, Annapolis, 1970).

54. Smith to Captain James Barron, May 15, 1807, in *Naval Documents . . . Barbary Powers*, VI, 524–525.

55. Paullin, *Diplomatic Negotiations*, 108–121; Allen, *Our Navy and the Barbary Corsairs*, 281–302; Irwin, *Diplomatic Relations*, 167–186; Wright and McLeod, *First Americans in North Africa*, 202–206; Guttridge and Smith, *The Commodores*, 272–283; Tucker; *Dawn Like Thunder*, 447–465. President Madison had written his Secretary of State James Monroe, "the Dey must distinctly understand that tho' [sic] we prefer peace we are prepared for war, and will make no change in the late treaty, nor concessions of any sort to avoid it." Madison to Monroe, June 25, 1816, quoted in Irwin, 184.

Bibliography

Adams, Henry, *History of the United States of America During the Administration of Thomas Jefferson* (4 vols, New York, 1901)

Albion, Robert G., "The First Days of the Navy Department," *Military Affairs,* XII (Spring 1948)

Albion, Robert G., *Forests and Sea Power: The Timber Problem of the Royal Navy, 1652–1862* (Cambridge, 1926)

Albion, Robert Greenhalgh, "Distant Stations," *U.S. Naval Institute Proceedings,* LXXX (March 1951)

Albion, Robert Greenhalgh and Pope, Jennie Barnes, *Sea Lanes in Wartime: The American Experience, 1775–1942* (New York, 1942)

Allen, Gardner W., *Our Navy and the Barbary Corsairs* (Reprint, Hamden, CT, 1965)

Allen, Gardner W., *Massachusetts Privateers of the Revolution* (Boston, 1927)

Allen, Gardner W., *A Naval History of the American Revolution* (2 vols, Boston, 1913)

Ammon, Harry, *The Genet Mission* (New York, 1973)

Anderson, William G., "John Adams, the Navy, and the Quasi-War With France," *The American Neptune,* XXX (April 1970)

Andrews, Charles M., *The Colonial Period of American History: England's Commercial and Colonial Policy* (4 vols, New Haven, 1934–1938)

Appleby, Joyce, "Commercial Farming and the 'Agrarian Myth' in the Early Republic," *Journal of American History,* 68 (March 1982)

Barnardo, C. Joseph, and Bacon, Eugene H., *American Military Policy: Its Development Since 1775* (Harrisburg, PA, 1955)

Bass, William P., "Who Did Design the First U.S. Frigates?," *Naval History* V (Summer 1991)

Bauer, Jack, "Naval Shipbuilding Programs 1794–1860," *Military Affairs,* 29 (Spring 1965)

Beaglehold, J. C., *The Life of Captain James Cook* (Stanford, 1974)

Beer, George Louis, *British Colonial Policy, 1754–1765* (New York, 1907)

Bell, Frederick J., *Room to Swing a Cat, or Tales of the Old Navy* (New York, 1938)

Bemis, Samuel Flagg, *The Diplomacy of the American Revolution* (New York, 1935)

Bemis, Samuel Flagg, *Jay's Treaty: A Study in Commerce and Diplomacy* (New York, 1924)

Bemis, Samuel Flagg, ed., *The American Secretaries of State and Their Diplomacy* (10 vols, New York, 1928)

Billias, George Athan, ed., *George Washington's Opponents: British Generals and Admirals in the American Revolution* (New York, 1964)

Billias, George Athan, ed., *George Washington's Generals* (New York, 1964)

Boudriot, Jean, *The Seventy-Four-Gun Ship* (4 vols, Annapolis, 1987–89)

Bowman, Albert Hall, *The Struggle for Neutrality: Franco-American Diplomacy During the Federalist Era* (Knoxville, 1974)

Boxer, Charles R., *The Portuguese Seaborne Empire, 1415–1825* (New York, 1969)

Boxer, Charles R., *The Dutch Seaborne Empire* (New York, 1965)

Bradford, James C., ed., *Command Under Sail: Makers of the American Naval Tradition, 1776–1850* (Annapolis, 1985)

Brant, Irving, *James Madison, Secretary of State, 1800–1809* (Indianapolis, 1953)

Brewington, Marion V., "American Naval Guns, 1775–1785," *The American Neptune,* III (January 1943); III (April 1943)

Brewington, Marion V., "The Design of our First Frigates," *The American Neptune,* VIII (1948)

Bridenbaugh, Carl, *Cities in the Wilderness: The First Century of Urban Life in America, 1625–1742* (New York, 1938)

Bridenbaugh, Carl, *Vexed and Troubled Englishmen 1590–1842* (New York, 1968)

Bryson, Thomas A., *American Diplomatic Relations With the Middle East, 1784–1975: A Survey* (Metuchen, NJ, 1977)

Burnett, Edmund Cody, *The Continental Congress* (New York, 1941)

Burnett, Edmund Cody, ed., *Letters of Members of the Continental Congress* (8 vols, Washington, 1921–1938)

Carr, James A., "John Adams and the Barbary Problem: The Myth and the Record," *The American Neptune,* XXVI (October 1966)

Carrigg, John J., "Benjamin Stoddert and the Foundations of the American Navy," (Ph.D. dissertation, Georgetown University, 1953)

Carroll, Charles F., *The Timber Economy of Puritan New England* (Providence, RI, 1974)

Chapelle, Howard I., *The History of American Sailing Ships* (New York, 1935)

Chapelle, Howard I., *The History of the American Sailing Navy: The Ships and Their Development* (New York, 1949)

Chapin, Howard M., *Privateer Ships and Sailors, The First Century of American Colonial Privateering, 1625–1725* (Toulon, 1926)

Chapin, Howard M., *Privateering in King George's War, 1739–1748* (Providence, RI, 1928)

Chidsey, Donald Barr, *The American Privateers* (New York, 1962)

Chinard, Gilbert, *Honest John Adams* (Boston, 1933)

Cipolla, Carlo M., *Guns, Sails, and Empires: Technological Innovation and the Early Phases of European Expansion, 1400–1700* (New York, 1966)

Clark, William Bell and Morgan, William James, eds., *Naval Documents of the American Revolution* (9 vols, Washington, 1964–1986)

Clark, William Bell, "American Naval Policy, 1775–1776," *The American Neptune,* I (1941)

Clark, William Bell, *George Washington's Navy: Being an Account of His Excellency's Fleet in New England Waters* (Baton Rouge, 1960)

Clark, William Bell, *Ben Franklin's Privateers: A Naval Epic of the American Revolution* (Baton Rouge, 1956)

Cochran, Thomas G., "The Business Revolution," *American Historical Review,* 79 (December 1974)

Coletta, Paolo E., ed., *American Secretaries of the Navy* (2 vols, Annapolis, 1980)

Commager, Henry Steele and Morris, Richard B., eds., *The Spirit of Seventy-Six: The Story of the American Revolution as Told by Participants* (2 vols, Indianapolis, 1958)

Commins, Saxe, ed., *Basic Writings of George Washington* (New York, 1948)

Cooper, James Fenimore, *History of the Navy of the United States of America* (2 vols, Philadelphia, PA, 1839)

Corbett, Julian S., *England in the Seven Years' War: A Study in Combined Strategy* (2 vols, London, 1907)

Cracknell, William R., Jr., "The Role of the U.S. Navy in Inshore Waters," *Naval War College Review,* 21 (November 1968)

Cross, A. L., "On Coppering Ship's Bottoms," *American Historical Review,* XXXIII (1927-1928)

Davies, George E., "Robert Smith and the Navy," *Maryland Historical Magazine,* XIV (December 1919)

Davis, Ralph, *The Rise of the Atlantic Economies* (Ithaca, NY, 1973)

de Madariaga, Isabel, *Britain, Russia and the Armed Neutrality of 1780: Sir James Harris's Mission to St. Petersburg During the American Revolution* (New Haven, 1962)

De Conde, Alexander, *The Quasi-War: The Politics and Diplomacy of the Undeclared War with France, 1797–1801* (New York, 1966)

De Conde, Alexander, *Entangling Alliance: Politics and Diplomacy under George Washington* (Durham, NC, 1958)

Deardon, Paul F., *The Rhode Island Campaign of 1778: Inauspicious Dawn of Alliance* (Providence, 1980)

Dewey, David Rich, *Financial History of the United States* (10th ed., New York, 1928)

Dickerson, Oliver M., *The Navigation Acts and the American Revolution* (Philadelphia, 1951)

Dowell, Vincent J., "The Birth of the American Navy," *U.S. Naval Institute Proceedings,* 81 (November 1955)

Dull, Jonathan, *The French Navy and the American Revolution: A Study of Arms and Diplomacy, 1774–1787* (Princeton, 1975)

Earle, Edward Mead, ed., *The Federalist: A Commentary on the Constitution of the United States* (New York, n.d.)

Ekirch, Arthur A., Jr., *The Civilian and the Military: A History of the American Antimilitarist Tradition* (New York, 1956)

Farrand, Max, ed., *The Records of the Federal Convention of 1787* (3 vols, New Haven, 1911)

Ferguson, Eugene S., *Truxton of the Constellation: The Life of Commodore Thomas Truxton, U.S. Navy, 1755–1778* (Baltimore, 1956)

Field, James A., Jr., *America and the Mediterranean World, 1776–1882* (Princeton, 1969)

Fiske, John, *The Critical Period* (Boston, 1888)

Ford, P. L., ed., *The Writings of Thomas Jefferson* (10 vols, New York, 1892–1899)

Fowler, William M., Jr., "Esek Hopkins: Commander-in-Chief of the Continental Navy," in Bradford, James C., ed., *Command Under Sail: Makers of the American Naval Tradition, 1776–1850* (Annapolis, 1985)

Gipson, Lawrence H., *The Great War for the Empire: The Culmination, 1760–1763* (Caxton, ID, and New York, 1969)

Gipson, Lawrence H., *The British Empire Before the American Revolution: The Triumphant Empire, 1763–1766* (New York, 1956)

Goodwin, A., ed., *The American and French Revolutions, 1763–93* (Cambridge, 1965)

Gordon, Maurice Bear, "Naval and Maritime Medicine During the Revolution," in Clark and Morgan, *Naval Documents of the American Revolution*, VI, Appendix A.

Gordon, Maurice Bear, *Naval and Maritime Medicine During the American Revolution* (Ventnor, NJ, 1978)

Graham, Gerald S., *The Politics of Naval Supremacy: Studies in British Maritime Ascendancy* (Cambridge, 1965)

Graham, Gerald S., *Empire of the North Atlantic: the Maritime Struggle for North America* (2nd ed., London, 1958)

Graham, Malbone W., *American Diplomacy in the International Community* (Baltimore, 1948)

Guttridge, Leonard and Smith, Jay D., *The Commodores: The U.S. Navy in the Age of Sail* (New York, 1969)

Habakkuk, H. J., "Population, Commerce and Economic Ideas," in A. Goodwin, ed., *The American and French Revolutions, 1763–93* (New Cambridge Modern History, Cambridge, 1965)

Hagan, Kenneth J., ed., *In Peace and War: Interpretations of American Naval History, 1775–1978* (Westport, CT, and London, 1978)

Harper, Lawrence A., *The English Navigation Laws: A Seventeenth-Century Experiment in Social Engineering* (New York, 1939)

Hayes, Frederic H., "John Adams and American Sea Power," *The American Neptune*, XXV (1965)

Henrich, Joseph G., "The Triumph of Ideology: The Jeffersonians and the Navy, 1779–1807," (Ph.D. dissertation, Duke University, 1971)

Hickey, Donald R., "Federalist Defense Policy in the Age of Jefferson, 1801–1812," *Military Affairs*, XLV (April 1981)

Higginbotham, Don, *The War of American Independence: Military Attitudes, Policies and Practice, 1763–1789* (New York, 1971)

Higgins, A. Pearce, "The Growth of International Law, Maritime Rights and Colonial Titles, 1648–1763," in *The Cambridge History of the British Empire, I, The Old Empire: From the Beginnings to 1763* (New York, 1929)

Hill, Charles E., "James Madison," in Bemis, ed., *American Secretaries of State*, III

Hyde, Charles Cheney, *International Law Chiefly as Interpreted and Applied by the United States* (3 vols, 2nd ed., Boston, 1951)

Hyneman, Charles S., "Neutrality During the European Wars of 1792–1815:

America's Understanding of Her Obligations," *American Journal of International Law,* XXIV (April 1930)

Irwin, Ray W., *The Diplomatic Relations of the United States with the Barbary Powers, 1776–1816* (Chapel Hill, NC, 1931)

Jackson, Melvin H., *Privateers in Charleston, 1793–1796: An Account of a French Palatinate in South Carolina* (Washington, 1969)

Jacobs, James Ripley, *The Beginnings of the U.S. Army, 1783–1812* (Princeton, 1947)

Jamieson, Alan G., "American Privateering in the Leeward Islands, 1776–1778," *The American Nepture,* XLIII (January 1938)

Jenkins, E. H., *A History of the French Navy, From Its Beginnings to the Present Day* (Annapolis, 1973)

Jensen, Merrill, *The New Nation: A History of the United States During the Confederation, 1781–1789* (New York, 1950)

Jessup, P. C., and Deak, F., *Neutrality: Its History, Economics and Law I: The Origins* (New York, 1935)

Jones, Robert F., "The Naval Thought and Policy of Benjamin Stoddert, First Secretary of the Navy, 1798–1801," *The American Neptune,* XXIV (January 1964)

Kelly, John Joseph, Jr., "The Struggle for American Seaborne Independence as Viewed by John Adams," (Ph.D. dissertation, U. of Maine, 1973)

Kimmel, Lewis H., *Federal Budget and Fiscal Policy, 1779–1958* (Washington, 1959)

Knight, R. J. B., "The Introduction of Copper Sheathing, 1778–1786," *Mariner's Mirror,* 59 (1973)

Knox, Dudley W., *The Naval Genius of George Washington* (Boston, 1932)

Knox, Dudley W., ed., *Naval Documents Related to the Quasi-War Between the United States and France: Naval Operations From February 1797 to December 1801* (7 vols, Washington, 1935–1938)

Knox, Dudley W., ed., *Naval Documents Related to the United States War with the Barbary Powers: Naval Operations Including Diplomatic Background From 1785 Through 1807* (7 vols, Washington, 1939–1946)

Kohn, Richard H., *Eagle and Sword: The Beginnings of the Military Establishment in America* (New York, 1975)

Lang, Daniel George, *Foreign Policy in the Early Republic: The Law of Nations and the Balance of Power* (Baton Rouge, 1985)

Lavery, Brian, *The Ship of the Line* (2 vols, Annapolis, 1984)

Leach, Douglas Edward, *Arms for Empire: A Military History of the British Colonies in North America, 1607–1763* (New York, 1973)

Lemish, Jesse, "Jack Tar in the Streets: Merchant Seamen in the Politics of

Revolutionary America," *William and Mary Quarterly*, Third Series, XXV, (July 1968)

Lewis, Michael, *Armada Guns: A Comparative Study of English and Spanish Armaments* (London, 1961)

Lewis, Michael, *The History of the British Navy* (Baltimore, 1957)

Lofgren, Charles A., "War-Making Under the Constitution: The Original Understanding," *The Yale Law Journal*, 81 (March 1982)

Long, David F., *Nothing Too Daring: A Biography of Commodore David Porter, 1783–1843* (Annapolis, 1970)

Long, David F., *Gold Braid and Foreign Relations: Diplomatic Activities of U.S. Naval Officers, 1798–1883* (Annapolis, 1988)

Long, David F., *Ready to Hazard: A Biography of Commodore William Bainbridge, 1774–1833* (Ann Arbor, MI, 1981)

Long, David F., *Sailor-Diplomat: A Biography of Commodore James Biddle, 1783–1848* (Boston, 1983)

Lovejoy, David S., *Rhode Island Politics and the American Revolution, 1760–1776* (Providence, RI, 1958)

Lower, Arthur R. M., *Great Britain's Woodyard: British America and the Timber Trade, 1763–1867* (Montreal, 1973)

Mackesy, Piers, *The War for America, 1775–1783* (Cambridge, MA, 1964)

Maclay, Edgar S., *A History of American Privateers* (New York, 1899)

MacLeod, Julia H., *The First American in North Africa: William Eaton's Struggle For a Vigorous Policy Against the Barbary Pirates, 1799–1805* (Princeton, 1945).

MacLeod, Julia H., "Jefferson and the Navy: A Defense," *Huntington Library Quarterly*, VIII (February 1945)

Mahan, Alfred Thayer, *Major Operations of the Navies in the War of American Independence* (Boston, 1913; reprint, New York, 1969)

Mahan, Alfred Thayer, *Naval Strategy, Compared and Contrasted with the Principles and Practices of Military Operations on Land* (Boston, 1911)

Mahan, Alfred Thayer, *The Influence of Sea Power Upon the French Revolution and Empire, 1793–1812* (2 vols, London, 1892)

Mahan, Alfred Thayer, *The Influence of Sea Power Upon History, 1660–1783* (Boston, 1890)

Mahan, Alfred Thayer, *Sea Power in its Relations to the War of 1812* (2 vols, Boston, 1905)

Malone, Dumas and Johnson, Allen, eds., *Dictionary of American Biography* (22 vols, New York, 1946)

Malone, Dumas, *Jefferson the President: First Term, 1801–1805* (Boston, 1970)

Malone, Dumas, *Jefferson and His Time: Jefferson the Virginian* (Boston, 1948)

Malone, Dumas, *Jefferson and the Rights of Man* (Boston, 1952)

Marcus, G. J., *A Naval History of England: The Formative Centuries* (Boston, 1961)

Marcus, G. J., *The Age of Nelson: The Royal Navy, 1793–1815* (New York, 1971)

Marks, Frederick Q., III, *Independence on Trial: Foreign Affairs and the Making of the Constitution* (Baton Rouge, 1973)

Mattingly, Garrett, *The Armada* (Boston, 1959)

Maurer, Maurer, "Coppered Bottoms for the Royal Navy: A Factor in the Maritime War of 1778–1783," *Military Affairs,* XIV (1950)

May, W. E. and Holder, Leonard, *A History of Marine Navigation* (New York, 1973)

McKee, Christopher, *Edward Preble: A Naval Biography, 1761–1807* (Annapolis, 1972)

McKee, Christopher, *A Gentlemanly and Honorable Profession: The Creation of the U.S. Naval Officer Corps, 1794–1815* (Annapolis, 1991)

Middleton, Richard, *The Bells of Victory: The Pitt-Newcastle Ministry and the Conduct of the Seven Years' War, 1757–1762* (Cambridge, 1985)

Miller, Nathan, *Sea of Glory: The Continental Navy Fights for Independence, 1775–1783* (New York, 1974)

Millett, Allan R., *Semper Fidelis: The History of the Marine Corps* (New York, 1980)

Morgan, William James, *Captains to the Northward: The New England Captains in the Continental Navy* (Barre, MA, 1959)

Morgan, William James, "The Pivot Upon Which Everything Turned: French Naval Superiority That Insured Victory at Yorktown," *The Ironworker,* 22 (Spring 1958)

Morison, Samuel Eliot, *The European Discovery of America: The Southern Voyages* (New York, 1974)

Morison, Samuel Eliot, *The European Discovery of America: The Northern Voyages* (New York, 1971)

Morison, Samuel Eliot, *John Paul Jones: A Sailor's Biography* (paperback, New York, 1964)

Morris, Richard B., *The Peacemakers: The Great Powers and American Independence* (New York, 1965)

Morris, Richard Valentine, *A Defense of the Conduct of Commodore Morris During His Command in the Mediterranean* (New York, 1804)

Morse, Sidney G., "State or Continental Privateers?", *American Historical Review,* LII (October 1946)

Morse, Sidney G., "The Fleet," *The American Neptune,* V (April 1945)

Nasatir, Abraham P., *Spanish War Vessels on the Mississippi, 1792–1796* (New Haven, 1968)

Naval History Division, *Maritime Dimensions of the American Revolution* (Washington, 1977)

Naval Regulations 1802 Issued by Command of the President of the United States (Reprint, Annapolis, 1970)

Naval History Division, *Dictionary of American Naval Fighting Ships* (8 vols, Washington, 1959–1991)

Nef, John U., *War and Human Progress: An Essay on the Rise of Industrial Civilization* (paperback ed., New York, 1968)

Nettles, Curtis P., "British Mercantilism and the Economic Development of the Thirteen Colonies," *The Journal of Economic History,* XII (Spring 1952)

Nevins, Agnes, *The Provincial Committee of Safety of the American Revolution* (Reprint, New York, 1968)

Pares, R., *Colonial Blockade and Neutral Rights, 1738–1763* (Boston, 1938)

Parry, John Horace, *The Age of Reconnaissance, 1460–1650* (New York, 1963)

Patterson, A. T., *The Other Armada: The Franco-Spanish Attempt to Invade Britain in 1779* (Manchester, 1960)

Paullin, Charles Oscar, *Commodore John Rodgers: Captain, Commodore and Senior Officer of the American Navy, 1773–1838* (Annapolis, 1909, 1967)

Paullin, Charles O., *Diplomatic Negotiations of the American Naval Officers, 1778–1888* (Reprint, Gloucester, MA, 1967)

Paullin, Charles Oscar, *Paullin's History of Naval Administration, 1775–1911: A Collection of Articles From the Naval Institute Proceedings* (Annapolis, 1968)

Paullin, Charles O., ed., *Out Letters of the Continental Marine Committee and Board of Admiralty* (2 vols, New York, 1914)

Paullin, Charles O., *American Voyages to the Orient, 1690–1865: An Account of Merchant and Naval Activities in China, Japan, and the Various Pacific Islands* (Annapolis, 1971)

Paullin, Charles Oscar, *Diplomatic Negotiations of American Naval Officers, 1778–1883* (Reprint, Gloucester, MA, 1967)

Paullin, Charles O., *The Navy of the American Revolution: Its Administration, Its Policy and Its Achievements* (Cleveland, 1906)

Pelzer, John D., "Armed Merchantmen and Privateers: Another Perspective on America's Quasi-War With France," *The American Neptune,* 50 (Fall 1990)

Powers, Stephen Tallichet, "The Decline and Extinction of American Naval Power, 1781–1787," (Ph.D. dissertation, U. of Notre Dame, 1965)

Pritchard, James, *Louis XV's Navy, 1748–1762: A Study of Organization and Administration* (Kingston, 1987)

Prucha, Paul, *The Sword of the Republic: The United States Army on the Frontier, 1783–1846* (New York, 1969)

Quinn, David Beers, *England and the Discovery of America, 1481–1620, From the Bristol Voyages of the Fifteenth Century to the Pilgrim Settlement at Plymouth: The Exploration, Exploitation, and Trial-and-Error Colonization of North America by the English* (New York, 1974)

Quinn, David Beers, and Ryan, A. N., *England's Sea Empire* (London & Boston, 1983)

Richardson, James D., ed., *A Compilation of the Messages and Papers of the Presidents* (20 vols, New York, 1923)

Richmond, Herbert, *The Navy as an Instrument of Policy, 1558–1727* (Cambridge, 1953)

Richmond, H. W., *National Policy and Naval Strength and Other Essays* (London, 1928)

Roberts, William R., and Sweetman, Jack, eds., *New Interpretations in Naval History: Selected Papers from the Ninth Naval History Symposium* (Annapolis, 1991)

Rodger, N. A. M., *The Wooden World: An Anatomy of the Georgian Navy* (Annapolis, 1986)

Rohr, John A., "Constitutional Foundations of the United States Navy," *Naval War College Review*, XLV (Winter 1992)

Roosevelt, Franklin D., "Our First Frigates. Some Unpublished Facts About Their Construction," *Transactions, Society of Naval Architects and Marine Engineers*, XII (1914)

Rowse, A. L., *The Elizabethans and America* (New York, 1959)

Sands, John O., *Yorktown's Captive Fleet* (Charlottesville, VA, 1983)

Savage, Carlton, ed., *Treaties, Conventions, International Acts, Protocols and Agreements Between the United States of America and Other Powers, 1776–1809* (2 vols, Washington, 1910)

Savageau, David LePere, "The United States Navy and Its 'Half War' Prisoners, 1798–1801," *The American Neptune*, XXXI (July 1971)

Savelle, Max, "The American Balance of Power and European Diplomacy 1713–78," in Richard B. Morris, ed., *The Era of the American Revolution* (New York, 1939)

Savelle, Max, *The Origins of American Diplomacy: The International History of Angloamerica, 1492–1763* (New York, 1967)

Scammell, G. V., *The World Encompassed: The First European Maritime Empires* (Berkeley, 1981)

Schaffel, Kenneth, "The American Board of War, 1776–1781," *Military Affairs,* 50 (October 1986)

Scheina, Robert L., "A Matter of Definition: A New Jersey Navy, 1777–1783," *The American Neptune,* XXXIX (July 1979)

Scheina, Robert L., "Benjamin Stoddert, Politics and the Navy," *American Mercury,* 35 (January 1976)

Shephard, James F., and Walter, Gary M., *Shipping, Maritime Trade and the Economic Development of Colonial North America* (New York, 1972)

Short, Lloyd Milton, *The Development of National Administrative Organization in the United States* (Baltimore, 1923)

Smelser, Marshall, "Whether to Provide and Maintain a Navy, 1787–1788," *U.S. Naval Institute Proceedings,* 83 (September 1957)

Smelser, Marshall, *The Congress Founds the Navy, 1787–1798* (Notre Dame, 1959)

Smith, Louis, *American Democracy and Military Power: A Study of Civil Control of the Military Power of the United States* (Chicago, 1951)

Sofaer, Abraham D., *War, Foreign Affairs and Constitutional Power: The Origins* (Cambridge, MA, 1976)

Spencer, William, *Algiers in the Age of the Corsairs* (Norman, OK, 1988)

Sprout, Harold and Sprout, Margaret, *The Rise of American Naval Power, 1776–1918* (Princeton, 1942)

Stinchcombe, William C., *The American Revolution and the French Alliance* (Syracuse, 1969)

Stinchcombe, William, *The XYZ Affair* (Westport, CT, 1980)

Stout, Neil R., *The Royal Navy in America: A Study of Enforcement of British Colonial Policy in the Era of the American Revolution, 1760–1776* (Annapolis, 1973)

Stout, Neil R., "Manning the Royal Navy in North America, 1763–1775," *The American Neptune,* XXIII (July 1963)

Stuart, Reginald C., *The Half-Way Pacifist: Thomas Jefferson's View of War* (Buffalo, 1978)

Symonds, Craig, "William S. Bainbridge: Bad Luck or Fatal Flaw," in Bradford, ed., *Command Under Sail: Makers of the American Naval Tradition, 1775–1850*

Symonds, Craig, "The Antinavalists: The Opponents of Naval Expansion in the Early National Period," *The American Neptune,* 39 (February 1979)

Symonds, Craig, *Navalists and Anti-Navalists: The Naval Policy Debate in the United States, 1785–1827* (Newark, DE, 1978)

Syrett, David, *The Royal Navy in American Waters, 1775–1783* (Brookfield, VT, 1989)

Syrett, David, "American and British Naval Historians and the American Revolutionary War, 1875–1980," *The American Neptune,* XLII (July 1982)

Tilley, John A., *The British Navy and the American Revolution* (Columbia, SC, 1987)

Tuchman, Barbara W., *The First Salute* (New York, 1988)

Tucker, Spencer C., "The Carronade," *U.S. Naval Institute Proceedings,* 99 (August 1973)

U.S. Congress, *American State Papers,* Class VI, *Naval Affairs* (4 vols, Washington, 1832)

Upton, Emory, *The Military Policy of the United States* (Washington, 1904)

Valle, James E., *Rocks and Shoals: Order and Discipline in the Old Navy, 1800–1861* (Annapolis, 1980)

Wallace, Willard W., "Benedict Arnold: Traitorous Patriot," in Billias, George Athan, ed., *George Washington's Generals* (New York, 1964)

Walsh, John Evangelist, *Night on Fire: The First Complete Account of John Paul Jones's Greatest Battle* (New York, 1978)

Ward, Harry M., *The Department of War, 1781–1795* (Pittsburg, 1962)

Weeden, William B., *Economic and Social History of New England, 1620–1789* (2 vols, reprint, New York, 1963)

Weigley, Russell F., *History of the United States Army* (New York, 1967)

Weigley, Russell F., *The American Way of War: A History of United States Military Strategy and Policy* (New York, 1973)

Whipple, A. B. C., *To the Shores of Tripoli: The Birth of the U.S. Navy and Marines* (New York, 1991)

White, Howard, *Executive Influence in Determining Military Policy in the United States* (2 vols, Urbana, IL, 1925)

White, Leonard D., *The Jeffersonians: A Study in Administrative History 1801–1809* (New York, 1951)

White, Leonard D., *The Federalists: A Study in Administrative History* (New York, 1948)

Willcox, William B., "The British Road to Yorktown: A Study in Divided Command," *American Historical Review,* LII (October 1946)

Williams, Judith Blow, *British Commercial Policy and Trade Expansion, 1760–1850* (New York, 1972)

Wilson, Gary E., "The First American Hostages in Moslem Nations, 1784–1789," *The American Neptune,* XLI (July 1981)

Wolf, John B., *The Barbary Coast: Algiers Under the Turks, 1500–1830* (New York, 1979)

Wright, Louis B., and MacLeod, Julie H., *The First Americans in North Africa: William Eaton's Struggle For a Vigorous Policy Against the Barbary Pirates, 1799–1805* (Princeton, 1945)

Young, Eleanor, *Forgotten Patriot: Robert Morris* (New York, 1950)

Zimmerman, James Fulton, *Impressment of American Seamen* (Reprint, Port Washington, NY, 1966)

Index

RAYMOND G. O'CONNOR is Professor of History, Emeritus, University of Miami. He served in the Navy in enlisted and officer status and retired prior to receiving his Ph.D. from Stanford University. He has authored a number of books and articles and has taught at universities in the United States and abroad. His home is in California.